Student Engagement and Information Literacy

edited by

Craig Gibson

Association of College and Research Libraries
A division of the American Library Association
Chicago 2006

The paper used in this publication meets the minimum requirements of American National Standard for Information Sciences–Permanence of Paper for Printed Library Materials, ANSI Z39.48-1992. ∞

Student engagement and information literacy / edited by Craig Gibson.
    p. cm.
  Includes bibliographical references and index.
  ISBN 0 8389 8388 X (alk. paper)
    1.   Information literacy   Study and teaching (Higher) 2.   Electronic information resource literacy Study and teaching (Higher) 3.   Libraries and students. 4.   School librarian participation in curriculum planning. 5. Motivation in education. 6. Teacher librarians. I. Gibson, Craig, 1954

  ZA3075.S78 2006

Printed on recycled paper.

Printed in the United States of America.

10 09 08 07 06   5 4 3 2 1

Table of Contents

Acknowledgments

It is one of the pleasures of editorship to offer thanks to those individuals who supported the editor in his work. I therefore want to acknowledge the support of Mary Jane Petrowski, Associate Executive Director of ACRL, and Mary Ellen Davis, Executive Director of ACRL, for their continued interest and unflagging belief in this book as it moved through myriad stages of development—from initial conceptualization, to suggestions about topics to be covered, to inquiries about progress. Their support has been indispensable and I am most grateful for their encouragement as this collection has come together to form a unified whole on the very timely topic of student engagement. I also want to thank Hugh Thompson, ACRL Publications Manager, for his expert assistance in the final stages of editing and production, and for his vital part in bringing this project to fruition.

I also want to acknowledge the support of my ACRL Immersion faculty colleagues, good friends and intellectual partners all, in the information literacy agenda to which we are dedicated. Their concern for, and belief in, student engagement has been an inspiring force.

I want to thank my wife, Lori, for many conversations about teaching and learning that center on student engagement. Her expertise and knowledge have been invaluable in helping me think about the shift to cultural dimensions of information literacy and student engagement.

Finally, I acknowledge my golden retriever, Macduff, who waited patiently by my desk as I edited and wrote. He provided many lighter moments during the editing process.

Introduction

This book offers librarians, faculty, technologists, assessment specialists, student development specialists, administrators, and others in the academy a variety of perspectives on the important issue of student engagement and how this dimension of learning connects with information literacy, increasingly recognized as an educational reform movement in its own right. Although "engagement" in all its permutations is currently very much on the minds of many in higher education—governing boards, legislatures, parents, and the public at large—the potential for creating a "multiplier effect" by linking it to a wide range of reform agendas and pedagogies is only beginning to be understood.

What is student engagement? Is this another fashionable term growing out of the most recent wave of education reform in higher education, destined to see its day and then fade from the consciousness of academic professionals and the general public? Or is it a set of benchmarks and indicators of student learning with staying power? Stephen Bowen, Senior Fellow of the Association of American Colleges and Universities, classifies student engagement in four ways that offer all in the academy a framework for understanding the concept more precisely and more comprehensively:

1. "student engagement with the learning process": that is, involvement through some form of active learning (the "pedagogies of engagement"—i.e, learning communities, writing-across-the-curriculum, service learning, field work, undergraduate research, case-based studies);

2. "student engagement with the object of study": exposing students to new concepts, facts, narratives, disciplinary frameworks, and having them construct knowledge of their own as a result;

3. "student engagement with contexts": that is, gaining additional breadth by adding other, complementary disciplinary frameworks,

and also gaining a sense of civic and societal responsibility—the ethical perspective—as a result of acquiring new knowledge;

4. "student engagement with the human condition": the widening of perspective focused on social and cultural challenges in all societies.[1]

These four types of engagement offer faculty, librarians, student life professionals, academic computing professionals, and deans and department chairs a way of thinking about students as whole persons; a clearer way of approaching curricular organization and reform, particularly drawing together curricular and cocurricular activities and projects for students; and a collaborative framework for tapping into reform energies, sometimes widespread and institutionalized, in other cases nascent and half-hidden, across the breadth of most college and university campuses. Explicit discussions of student engagement using such a framework can organize the academic enterprise in ways that transcend disciplinary-, departmental-, school-, and unit-based silos.

Information Literacy: An Unfolding Matrix

We are gaining a much clearer picture of the activities associated with student learning through the National Survey of Student Engagement (NSSE); at the same time, we are realizing the richness of the expanding array of abilities known as information literacy and related concepts such as information fluency and ICT (information and communication technology) skills. Our earlier (and limited) conception of information literacy as a set of skills or abilities is now evolving into a deepened re-conception of information literacy as a way of thinking, a dispositional habit, and a cultural practice.

First, information literacy is a *way of thinking* rather than a set of skills (as is aptly captured in the chapter title by Randy Hensley, one of the contributors here). It is a matrix of critical and reflective capacities, as well as disciplined creative thought, that impels the student to range widely through the information environment, forming initial hypotheses, collecting information sources and data, testing and retesting search paths, formulating and reinventing search strategies recursively, and applying rigorous standards to both the information found and the adaptive search process itself. Information literacy as a *way of thinking* is a constructive process, a dynamic, metacognitive drive, assisted by "scaffolding" provided by faculty, librarians, and others to create new understandings, new knowledge, and personal growth. When sustained through a supportive learning environment at course, program, or institutional level, information literacy can become a *dispositional habit*[2]—those affective tendencies to persist, overcome difficulties, to adapt to changing digital and print environments, to reach across disciplinary boundaries to solve information problems, to inquire deeply both within disciplines and beyond them, and to form a "habit of mind" that seeks ongoing improvement and self-discipline in inquiry, research, and integration of knowledge from varied sources. Finally, information literacy becomes a collective enterprise in the academy through a set of *cultural practices*. The phenomenon known as "legitimate peripheral participation,"[3] posited by Lave and Wenger, explains how novices in a new environment acquire expertise gradually by observing how experts think, talk, and practice their profession; through a process of acculturation, novices are slowly brought into "inner circle" of professional expertise and become full members of the community, having learned the practices, specialized vocabulary, norms, and values of the experts. This process of apprenticeship is evident in some curricular innovations in the academy, notably learning communities, undergraduate research, and service learning; participating in apprenticeship-like environments takes students to a new plane of thinking, acting, and being information-literate professionals. Another cultural feature of innovative learning environments, the "community of practice,"[4] as discussed by Wenger, Brown, Duguid, and others, offers the potential to reacculturate the academy with wider participation among faculty, librarians, students, technologists, and others in spontaneously generated interest groups focused on compelling issues—new conversations occurring outside formal organization structures and create grass-roots energies for reform of the curriculum, improvement in student life, and enhancing the learning environment throughout the academy. Information literacy becomes central to the "learning culture" when individual students, faculty, and librarians see how individual ways of thinking, collective dispositional habits, and cultural practices begin to merge beyond the individual, course, departmental, or program levels into a pervasive feature of an academic community.

When viewed through the lens of student engagement, information literacy can be understood as a developmental, dynamic maturing of intellect, passion, curiosity, inquiry, through involvement with both traditional academic coursework and with personal, professional, and civic responsibilities. Such ways of thinking, dispositional habits, and cultural practices obviously employ *skills,* some of which might still be usefully called "library skills" or "technology skills," but information literacy taps into deeper springs of mental and affective energies in the student. When linked with the "pedagogies of engagement" described by Bowen, information literacy becomes a property of the student as whole person, a way of being and interacting with an information-rich environment instead of an unintegrated skill set that can be casually employed to get a "quick fix" through use of a search engine. Information literacy is not a fixed or static phenomenon; rather, it is a self-renewing panoply of capacities, using critical thinking, metacognitive strategies, and, perhaps most important, creative abilities, dispositions, and native talents to foster self-motivation, to construct new knowledge, to build up expertise, and to acquire wisdom.[5] With this self-renewing, unfolding matrix of capacities, so congruent with the classic ideals of liberal education, students gain more facility and confidence with information, research, and knowledge building in a very uncertain, fluid information environment. In thinking of information literacy across the life span, we can see how crucial "engagement" or the affective or valuing components of learning are; the self-motivating, self-renewing dimensions of engaged learning go to very core of lifelong learning, a concept often linked with information literacy.

The wellsprings of information literacy therefore draw on the engagement of students with the totality of their surroundings, physical and virtual: with multiple disciplines, multiple academic and nonacademic environments, varied interactions with faculty and peers, with diverse information sources, with a constantly recalibrated set of learning challenges—and with vital research questions connecting academic knowledge with campus, community, and societal applications. Learning environments that create the best conditions for engaged information literacy are built up as an organic part of the entire culture across campus, through widespread adoption of the "pedagogies of engagement" and a reacculturation of all the relationships in the academy, with student learning and student engagement placed at the center of all organizational structures and curricular frameworks.

The affective component of information literacy has been the "missing link" in many discussions of the concept, and student engagement indicators established by the NSSE reveal why. In its *disengaged,* library-centric form (usually still referred to as "bibliographic instruction" or "library skills"), information literacy does not offer sufficient academic challenge or interest; may not offer sufficient active learning because of the limited impact of "one-shot" sessions; may not locate information literacy centrally in faculty–student interactions; may not be linked with other enriching educational experiences across the campus; and may not blend with other campus support systems. Too, *The Information Literacy Competency Standards for Higher Education*, a set of curricular guidelines and program planning guideposts, is heavily focused on the purely cognitive aspects of information retrieval, evaluation, management, and ethics, with occasional glances at valuing or affective elements. Many librarians, faculty, and their colleagues in the academy are searching for a more comprehensive framework for information literacy. Reframing the cognitive dimensions of information literacy, traditionally understood, within the energizing forces of student engagement as associated with benchmarks of the total learning environment (the learning culture or "engaged campus"), offers the power of the "multiplier effect" of two reform agendas merged into one.

Perspectives

The chapters in this book, written by two administrators, four faculty members, three librarians, and a professional association vice-president, offer a range of possibilities for thinking about student engagement and information literacy as mutually reinforcing reform agendas. In the first chapter, James Elmborg discusses John Dewey's *Democracy and Education* as a manifesto for educational change, describing Dewey's philosophy as focused on student "growth" as the key to progressive (unfolding) education for the life span. It is uncanny how this seminal work by Dewey anticipates so many of the recent debates in educational reform, and academic professionals concerned with the active learning and the full range of the "pedagogies of engagement" can productively trace the lineage of their ideas to Dewey. Elmborg identifies early, anticipatory linkages between student engagement and information literacy; his chapter provides a "frame" for subsequent chapters that presents different models for student engagement and exemplars of such engagement through case studies.

The second chapter, by Adrianna Kezar, presents the role of the librarian as central to student engagement through a review of data from national focus groups with librarians on their use of NSSE (National Survey of Student Engagement) at their institutions. This chapter provides a more specific "framing" for the following case-study-based chapters. In Chapter 3, Margit Watts focuses on service learning, one of the "pedagogies of engagement," as a strategy for realizing the classic goals of liberal education through student growth, thereby providing powerful motivating energy for information literacy. This chapter can be read productively with chapter 4 by Randy Hensley, not only because Watts and Hensley work at the same institution (University of Hawaii—Manoa) and have collaborated on information literacy and programming for student research skills, but also because they present an integrated view of information literacy, embedded in service learning (in Watt's chapter), as well as in learning communities linked with writing, disciplinary content, and service learning (Hensley's chapter).

Chapters 5 and 6 offer complementary perspectives on contemporary students and their values, attitudes, and characteristics. In chapter 5, Pat Maughan examines characteristics of NetGen or Millennial students and discusses implications for educating these students through the lens of recent higher education reform reports, particularly those focusing on accountability. Maughan discusses briefly the Mellon Library/Faculty Fellowship project at UC Berkeley and explores the implications of changing practices in teaching and learning for academic libraries. Jo Ann Carr, in chapter 6, also explores education reform, but from the perspective of the "disconnect" between K–12 and college and university pedagogies, and the attendant challenges in creating articulation for information literacy and student engagement between these two major levels of our educational system. Carr's chapter also addresses generational differences in learning between students and college faculty, as well as the implications of those differences for information literacy and resource-based learning. She suggests ways of providing articulation that transcend those differences.

Chapters 7 and 8 offer two case studies that show how student engagement and information literacy can coalesce in innovative curricular programming. In chapter 7, Nancy Shapiro and Kathy McAdams of the University of Maryland discuss "Discovery Projects," an undergraduate research, project-based curriculum for sophomores, in which students use primary source materials to engage significant research questions over a sustained period, process-oriented approach that places student inquiry at the heart of learning. In chapter 8, Darren Cambridge of George Mason University reviews another curricular innovation, linking service learning with learning communities, to give students the experience of seeking and using information in nonprofit community organizations. Cambridge expands traditional "academic" notions of information literacy to show how an "information ecology" manifested in organizational settings provides an optimal learning environment for developing information literacy capacity.

Chapter 9, by Joan Lippincott of the Coalition for Networked Information, gives a brief overview of learning communities and shows how technologies can support them, creating a greater sense of student engagement within those communities. Lippincott specifically discusses games, simulations, virtual worlds, and "learning spaces" in libraries as technology-enhanced environments that create conditions for engagement, motivation, and fluent use of information resources.

These chapters present a range of perspectives on engagement and information literacy, with a variety of pedagogies, learning environments, curricular structures, and institutional settings. Common themes surface throughout, however: the imperative to cross fixed or static boundaries among faculty, librarians, computing professionals, assessment specialists, and administrators, so that genuine collaboration can occur; the urgency of addressing core values about learning; the need to transform the curriculum so that classic goals of liberal education are linked with disciplinary learning, community involvement, and lifelong learning—with information literacy as a catalyst for sparking this transformation; and throughout, the need to "build capacity"—in student growth, in intra-institutional collaborations, and in revitalized curricula. This increased capacity, both individual and institutional, creates conditions for blending the classic liberal education ideal with the intense practicality of information literacy as catalyzing agent for campus, civic, and professional involvement. The authors of these chapters offer windows on engagement gained through the "wisdom of practice"[6] and thereby engage all of us, as readers, in an enlightened consideration of our own commitments to reform and innovation in the academy.

Notes

1. Stephen Bowen, "Engaged Learning: Are We All on the Same Page?" *Peer Review* [Association of American Colleges and Universities] 7, no. 2 (winter 2005). Available online from http://www.aacu.org/peerreview/pr-wi05/pr-wi05feature1.cfm.

2. My thinking here about the merging of information literacy as "way of thinking" into a "dispositional habit" has been greatly influenced by the research of Shari Tishman, Eileen Jay, and David Perkins. Their work on "thinking dispositions"

is very pertinent to any discussion of the affective dimensions of information literacy and learning in general. A representative paper is: Shari Tishman, Eileen Jay, and D.N. Perkins, "Teaching Thinking Dispositions: From Transmission to Enculturation." [MacArthur Foundation Grant Project, 1992]. Available online http://learnweb. harvard.edu/alps/thinking/docs/article2.html.

3. Jean C. Lave and Etienne Wenger, *Situated Learning: Legitimate Peripheral Participation* (New York: Cambridge University Pr. 1991).

4. Etienne Wenger, *Communities of Practice* (New York: Cambridge University Pr. 1998); John Seely Brown and Paul Duguid, "Organizational Learning and Communities-of-Practice: Toward a Unified Theory of Working, Learning, and Innovation," *Organization Science* 2 (1).

5. Christine Bruce, *The Seven Faces of Information Literacy* (Adelaide, Australia: AUSLIB Press, 1997). Bruce's summary of ethnographic research in this study shows how varying conceptions of information literacy deepen into true engagement as some aspects of information literacy become "foregrounded" and others become less important.

6. Lee Shulman, *The Wisdom of Practice: Essays on Teaching, Learning, and Learning to Teach* (San Francisco: Jossey-Bass, 2004). Shulman's essays are especially pertinent to librarians and their faculty colleagues who seek a collaborative scholarship of teaching, centering on student engagement.

The Other Dewey: John Dewey's *Democracy and Education* and Information Literacy

James Elmborg

John Dewey wrote *Democracy and Education* in a time of social and national transition to the modern age, a time with promises and concerns very much like those of our own time. Published in 1916, the book is set at the beginning of the twentieth century, and all the progress and problems of that century are palpably present. A series of social, scientific, and technical advancements forced reconsideration of many previously settled questions. In telecommunications, the telegraph and the telephone had revolutionized the way people could communicate across time and space. The newspaper had evolved into a powerful information resource that was nearly ubiquitous, if occasionally somewhat unreliable. Waves of immigrants had arrived at the shores of the United States (Swedish, Jewish, Italian, German, Japanese, most prominently), challenging the resources of the cities and settled notions of culture and nationality. A world war loomed just beyond the horizon. On a deeper and more philosophical level, Darwin, Freud, Marx, and Heisenberg had upended conventional wisdom, especially about the human capacity for reason and its usefulness as a way to comprehend and direct action in the physical world.

In this context, John Dewey aimed *Democracy and Education* (and much of his other work) directly at the public sphere and its anxieties. Dewey was a public intellectual who felt it was his duty to engage the citizenry in discussions of public importance. In *Democracy and Education*, he intended to create a compelling vision for public education. At the heart of that vision is the democratic citizen, educated for participation in a democratic society. Dewey envisioned these citizens as intellectually and physically engaged in creating a better world through intelligent action, and he imagined an education that could teach students to be such citizens. Almost a century later, as we imagine information literacy as a core educational concept with implications for both the library and more broadly conceived educational initiatives, we can find in Dewey a way of understanding its importance within the context of our evolving national experiment with democracy.

Dewey as Public Philosopher

For Dewey, education is inherently both philosophical and political. He argues that "education proceeds ultimately from the patterns furnished by [a society's] institutions, customs, and laws."[1] The central claim of the book rests on this assumption—that education is not "value neutral" but, rather, is inextricably related to the values and goals of its society. A democratic society requires an educational system designed specifically to educate its young people for the demands of democratic citizenship. In Dewey's view, no society had heretofore attempted to construct such an educational system. Dewey provides a history of educational philosophy, beginning with Plato and the Greeks, who recognized that "society is stably organized when each individual is doing that for which he has aptitude by nature in such a way as to be useful to others."[2] This seemingly egalitarian approach to education was in reality narrowed because "the [Greek] society in which the theory was propounded was so undemocratic that [Plato] could not work out a solution for the problem whose terms he clearly saw." Plato saw humans as dominated by certain inherent dispositions, some governed by "appetites" and others by a "courageous disposition." The former became members of the "laboring and trading class"; the latter became "citizen-subjects," defenders of the state in war and internal guardians in peace. A small number of citizens showed the aptitude to be philosophers, and these became the legislators of the society.

Plato's need to fit all citizens into one of three available social categories makes the Greek system simple, but relatively useless for a society based on unlimited human roles and potentials for its citizens.

In Dewey's view, educational theory was dominated by authoritarian approaches until the eighteenth century, when Rousseau argued that laws derived from social convention were inherently corrupting. Rousseau encouraged citizens to embrace their natural selves and to learn from and through nature rather than social convention. The social order embodied in Plato's world view became an evil to be transcended, and Rousseau advocated that citizens embrace their "humanity" and "human nature." Rousseau's followers were devoted "to emancipation of life from external restrictions, which operated to the exclusive advantage of the class to whom a past feudal system consigned power." Indeed, "natural law" could sweep away the corrupt institutions of society and institute a new natural order in harmony with each person's native instincts and abilities.[3] As Dewey notes, "as soon as the first enthusiasm for freedom waned, the weakness of the theory upon the constructive side became obvious. Merely to leave everything to nature was, after all, but to negate the very idea of education."[4] Education is by definition an intentional process designed to improve on random chance in learning. Dewey's constructive philosophy, far from haphazard, advocates a careful structuring and sequencing of knowledge to build understanding in students. The two extremes posited by Plato (to construct an educational system to serve the class system) and Rousseau (to let nature teach students "natural law" without an effort to structure learning) must somehow be navigated for a democratic education to occur.

In the nineteenth century, a subsequent evolution in educational theory began to unfold that, for Dewey, holds "incalculable significance for subsequent movements."[5] In this next incarnation,

> Under the influence of German thought in particular, education became a civic function and the civic function was identified with the realization of the ideal of the national state. The "state" was substituted for humanity; cosmopolitanism gave way to nationalism. To form the citizen, not the "man" became the aim of education.[6]

With this evolution, the aims of education became tied to the goals of the nation state, with the idea that a society could direct its evolution by the way it educates its citizens. The shift in emphasis away from "nature" as an ideal in itself toward a view of humans as participants in the survival and growth of the nation implied what Dewey calls "subordination of the individuals to the superior interest of the state both in military defense and in struggles for international supremacy in commerce."[7] As Dewey notes, the shift toward pragmatic, social definitions of education had profound implications for curriculum and pedagogy. One such effect is that "educational process was taken to be one of disciplinary training rather than of personal development."[8] This "disciplining" of the individual toward the good of the state had to be resolved to the satisfaction of the individual, which was accomplished by redefining what we mean by individual growth. In the German model, "the individual in his isolation is nothing; only in and through an absorption of the aims and meaning of organized institutions does he attain true personality. What appears to be his subordination to political authority and the demand for sacrifice of himself to the commands of his superiors is in reality but making his own the objective reason manifested in the state—the only way in which he can become truly rational."[9] Rather than pursuing perfect knowledge, students are expected to grow into good citizens, and education is charged with managing that growth. How we define good citizens depends on the values and aspirations of the state—its "social construction" of citizenship.

Dewey ends this chronology of educational philosophy by bringing this history to bear on America and its fledgling democracy. As Dewey notes, "the peculiarity of human life is that man has to create himself by his own voluntary efforts; he has to make himself a truly moral, rational, and free being."[10] It is in the interests of society to facilitate this growth and to thereby provide a "better future for humanity." Education conceived as a national project might imply this noble goal, but, in reality, "each generation is inclined to educate its young so as to get along in the present world instead of with a view to the proper end of education; the promotion of the best possible realization of humanity as humanity."[11] Herein lies the primary challenge for Dewey in *Democracy and Education*. As we experiment in a new form of society called "democracy," we must confront antiquated definitions of knowledge and education that perpetuate class systems and reify outmoded concepts of knowledge. We must imagine a future that does not exist and use education as the means for building that future. Most important, we must harmonize the goals of the nation with the goals of the individual so that they become one and the same goal. Indeed, Dewey argues, "one of the fundamental problems of education in and for a democratic society is set by the conflict of a nationalistic and a wider social aim."[12] More pointedly, he asks whether it is "possible for an educational system to be conducted by a national state and yet the full social ends of the educative process not be restricted, constrained, and corrupted?"[13]

Dewey's answer to this challenge is Progressive Education. The term has been used in many ways and has developed many connotations, but Dewey uses it quite literally. To educate students for democracy, we must educate them to deal for a future we do not (and cannot) know. Democratic life is unfolding (progressing) and a democratic education must therefore be an education in thinking through complex problems, developing the mind toward specific aims and goals, and learning to be reflective about the paths we choose. By focusing on these habits of mind (rather than on "content"), we educate students to "progress" through an unknown and unknowable future.

Literacy and Citizenship
Dewey defines education for democracy as "progressive" and "constructive" (two words that dominate *Democracy and Education*). This definition puts emphasis on the learner as the site of the educational process. Dewey's constructive metaphors involve "building" and "growth." These emphases put pressure on curriculum and pedagogy to develop new approaches that nurture what might be called the "new citizen." One primary difference between education for democracy and other, previous aims of education is its emphasis on creating citizens who can thrive in the open-ended climate of democracy rather than citizens who accept their inherited status as a social condition. As Dewey notes, "a democracy is more than a form of government, it is primarily a mode of associated living, of conjoint communicated experience. The extension in space of the number of individuals who participate in an interest so that each has to refer his own action to that of others, and to consider the action of others to give point and direction to his own, is equivalent to the breaking down of those barriers of class, race, and national territory which kept men from perceiving the full import of their activity."[14]

In a remarkably modern sounding caution, he argues that "a democratic criterion requires us to develop capacity to the point of competency to choose and make its own career. This principle is violated when the attempt is made to fit individuals in advance for definite industrial callings, selected not on the basis of trained original capacities, but on that of the wealth or social status of parents."[15] Charging education with social consciousness, Dewey argues that "it is the aim of progressive education to take part in correcting unfair privilege and unfair deprivation, not to perpetuate them."[16] The accompanying goal for curriculum and pedagogy then shifts to the development of a type of person—one who can adapt quickly to change, one who is able to participate in commerce and conversation with all fellow citizens, and one who can share intelligently in mutual governance. The school's job, he argues, is "to see to it that each individual gets an opportunity to escape from the limitations of the social group in which he was born, and to come into living contact with a broader environment."[17] "The intermingling in the school of different races, differing religions, and unlike customs," he continues, "creates for all a new and broader environment."[18] This new environment is a key element of the democracy envisioned by Dewey.

Dewey places a great deal of faith in the capacity for individuals to learn from each other, and he sees first schools and then the workplace as the primary settings for this "new and broader environment" to be created. School and work are the primary social contexts for people of diverse backgrounds to learn and solve problems together. In today's educational climate, lifelong learning is posited as one key to sustaining employability in a rapidly evolving marketplace, a fact Dewey acknowledges in noting that "industry has ceased to be essentially an empirical, rule-of-thumb procedure, handed down by custom. Its technique is now technological."[19] Education must prepare people to cope with this shift to technical industry, and Dewey embraces the challenge to educate for the workplace, noting that "an occupation is a continuous activity having a purpose. Education through occupations consequently combines within itself more of the factors conducive to learning than any other method."[20] Dewey warns, however, of a pernicious split, or "dualism," in our thinking about vocations, one that he finds peculiarly undemocratic. "Liberal culture," he notes, "has been linked to the notions of leisure, purely contemplative knowledge and a spiritual activity not involving the active use of bodily organs."[21] This education for liberal culture has therefore become the education of the elite, ruling class—for those whose lives are intellectual and spiritual, rather than manual.

As a result, "education which has to do chiefly with preparation for the pursuit of conspicuous idleness, for teaching, and for literary callings, and for leadership, has been regarded as non-vocational and even as peculiarly cultural."[22] This "dualism" creates one class of people (the "liberally cultured") who are contemplative and spiritual and who do not "labor," and another class of people (the working class) trained for vocations that are purely physical and "uncultured." Dewey notes that in "an autocratically managed society, it is often a conscious object to prevent the development of freedom and responsibility; a few do the planning and ordering, the others follow directions and are deliberately confined to narrow and prescribed channels of endeavor."[23] This kind of society is, of course, the antithesis of democracy. Dewey's solution to this dilemma is worth quoting at length:

> The only alternative is that all the earlier preparation for vocations be indirect rather than direct; namely through engaging interests of the pupil at the time. Only in this way can there be on the part of the educator and of the one educated a genuine discovery of personal aptitudes so that the proper choice of a specialized pursuit in later life may be indicated. Moreover, the discovery of capacity and aptitude will be a constant process as long as growth continues. It is a conventional and arbitrary view which assumes that discovery of the work to be chosen for adult life is made once for all at some particular date."[24]

Indeed, as we think about the implications of information literacy as a transformative movement in higher education, Dewey's emphasis on student engagement as the key to learning provides a centralizing perspective. For citizens to remain actively involved in their own governance and the structuring of their own lives and careers, they must be engaged early with issues that concern them. They must develop habits of mind that involve them in learning and growing and continuing to engage these issues for their entire lives.

Throughout *Democracy and Education*, Dewey argues that our classifying impulse that splits experience and the world into "dualisms" creates an artificial world for education. We split knowledge into "disciplines," conceive of the "mind" as a separate domain from the body, split experience into "lessons," and, most damagingly, separate our citizens into classes based on economy and standards we have written to enact our dualisms. Dewey argues that overcoming these dualisms to give students a holistic experience should be the central work of education. He concludes that "the educative process is its own end, and ... the only sufficient preparation for later responsibilities comes by making the most of immediate present life."[25] Democratic education must strive to overcome these dualisms and to educate students toward growth and reflection, for both life and work.

Growth as the Goal of Education

Dewey presents "growth" as the goal of education. He resists attaching a further goal to learning, arguing that "there is nothing to which growth is relative save more growth." By extension, he argues that "there is nothing to which education is subordinate save more education."[26] This allows him to define education in very straightforward terms: "education means the enterprise of supplying the conditions which insure growth."[27] Much of *Democracy and Education* flows from this central definition, which is closely related to the notion of the "progressive," and Dewey sees the structuring of experience to facilitate growth as key to progressive pedagogy. He argues that the "need of preparation for a continually developing life is great." Therefore, "it is imperative that every energy should be bent to making the present experience as rich and significant as possible. Then the present merges insensibly into the future and the future is taken care of."[28] For Dewey, learning is a habit of mind formed in youth through instruction and then becomes the foundation for a process of growth that continues on for the life of the person. Today's emphasis on lifelong learning derives directly from Dewey's description of learning as a lifelong process of growth.

The key to conducting school on the democratic model is to focus on structuring experience so that students maximize what they learn by working together productively to build knowledge for themselves. Rather than conveying "content" to the learner (which Dewey calls "pouring in learning") , the teacher's job is to structure experiences so that students grow and develop in desired directions. Dewey provides a "technical definition" of education: "that reconstruction or reorganization of experience which adds to the meaning of experience, and which increases ability to direct the course of subsequent experience."[29] Experience itself should not be haphazard, but carefully conceived. Ideally, "experience as an active process occupies time and...its later period completes its earlier portion; it brings to light connections involved, but hitherto unperceived. The later outcome thus reveals the meaning of the earlier whereas the experience as a whole establishes a bent or disposition toward the things possessing this meaning."[30]

Dewey argues against the Platonic notion of content as existing in pure forms outside the mind, and he argues against the development of pure abilities, aptitudes, or faculties within the mind. Education is, instead, "the formation of mind by setting up certain associations or connections of content by means of a subject matter presented from without." Education is thus "a building into the mind from without."[31]

Teachers must be able to structure experience in productive ways for students by consciously facilitating student growth, rather than transmitting content. Indeed, they should be experts in structuring experience to build understanding. "The business of the educator," Dewey suggests, "is, first, to select the proper material in order to fix the nature of the original reactions, and, secondly, to arrange the sequence of subsequent presentations on the basis of the store of ideas secured by prior transactions."[32] This way of describing education as "building" and "structuring" relates closely to what educational theorists call constructivism. Dewey's description of the way ideas are designed to build on each other is what constructivists call "scaffolding," the activation of prior schemes of thinking so that new experiences can become coherent based on past knowledge. Any new concept "interacts with the contents already submerged below consciousness [and] the first thing is the step of 'preparation'—that is, calling into special activity and getting above the floor of consciousness those older presentations which are to assimilate the new one. Then after the presentation, [the teacher should] follow the processes of interaction of new and old; then comes the application of the newly formed content to the performance of some task."[33] This general process generates "growth," as students learn to build on past experiences and, most important, to solve problems by learning what is involved in the solving. Throughout this process, Dewey advocates that we use real human experience for the basis of instruction. By isolating scholastic work from experience in the world, we sever connections that should be the foundation for the learning process. Dewey's approach provides a methodology for general education. He notes that "isolation of subject matter from social context is the chief obstruction in current practice to securing a general training of mind. Literature, art, religion, when thus dissociated, are just as narrowing as the technical things which the professional upholders of general education strenuously oppose."[34]

The pedagogy most appropriate to the development of student-citizens in the pursuit of general education is "collaborative learning." By structuring experience so that students work together on problems, they learn the skills they will need to function as equal citizens in the democratic process. They learn to respect each other's talents and efforts, they learn to appreciate the whole of the problem while contributing to its solving, and they contribute to the building of knowledge in each other. Dewey expresses concern over both pedagogical and workplace approaches based on scientific management principles. He acknowledges that "efficiency in production often demands division of labor." However, such approaches are "reduced to a mechanical routine unless workers see the technical, intellectual, and social relationships involved in what they do."[35] Moreover, when labor (educational or workplace) is divided into discrete parts without regard for understanding how the parts constitute a whole, the result is that people develop "an antisocial spirit" that is "found wherever one group has interests 'of its own.'"[36] For Dewey, this "cliquish" tendency signals a failure of democracy and education to function as it should.

Much of the rhetoric surrounding education today is based on bringing business principles to the management of schools. To the extent that business models enact egalitarian practices that encourage learning on the job, upward mobility, and involve all participants in democratic management, Dewey would probably agree with that impulse. However, much of current business practice works on distinctly undemocratic principles, creating rigid class structures between management and labor and focusing on the mastery of skills in workers rather than human growth and development. The outsourcing of discrete production tasks to workers who never see the final product is antithetical to Dewey's vision of how work can bring meaning and structure to democratic life. To the extent that schools surrender their focus on developing humans and focus, instead, on developing workers who fit into this model, we fail our students and we fail our society. Dewey worries that when education focuses on creating workers, "its prevailing purpose is the protection of what it has got, instead of reorganization and progress through wider relationships."[37] For these reasons, the primary threat to democracy enacted through education is the looming concern that business interests will invade education and orient the pedagogy and curriculum toward the training of workers in isolated skills, rather than a whole education for participation in our experiment in democratic citizenship.

Information Overload

Dewey does not use the term information literacy in *Democracy and Education* (a fact that should surprise no one). He is concerned, however, with information and its role in the educational process. In general, information without context is meaningless in Dewey's educational process. He notes that "in schools there is usually both too much and too little information supplied by others. The accumulation and acquisition of information for purposes of reproduction in recitation and examination is made too much of."[38] The danger in viewing information in this way is that it ceases to function in the process of growth outlined above. When accumulating information becomes an "end in itself,... then the goal becomes to heap it up and display it when called for."[39] Dewey refers to this method of using information in the educational process as "cold-storage," and he finds it "inimical to educative development."[40] Information "heaped up" for later use tends to clutter students' minds, and this clutter creates obstacles to their thinking. Such students "have no practice in selecting what is appropriate, and no criterion to go by; everything is on the same dead static level."[41] On the other hand, Dewey recognizes the value of information when it functions "in experience through use in application to the student's own purposes." In such cases, he suggests, there would be "need of more varied resources in books, pictures, and talks than are usually at command."[42] Information in and of itself has no inherent value. It can be used to "clutter" students' minds, or it can be used as a crucial part of knowledge building.

Dewey provides a series of questions "for estimating the value of educational material in school. Does it grow naturally out of some question with which the student is concerned? Does it fit into his more direct acquaintance so as to increase its efficacy and deepen its meaning? If it meets these two requirements, it is educative."[43] These key questions provide a framework for thinking about information literacy. Information can be "heaped up" in and for itself, but such an approach is not educative. Information must function in real ways to be educative: a real question must drive the search, and the information must effectively address the question and deepen its meaning. Dewey notes that there is no "right amount" of information. Indeed, "the more, the better, provided the student has a need for it and can apply it in some situation of his own."[44] However, he cautions that "information severed from thoughtful action is dead, a mind-crushing load."[45] Students need to find the right kinds of information to use in defining thoughtful, goal-oriented action. Instruction should help them learn to do so.

Rather than focus on information, instruction should be designed to promote thinking. Information does, of course, have an important role in thinking. It can provide "suggestions, inferences, conjectured meanings, suppositions, tentative explanations—ideas, in short."[46] These provide a context for thinking, but as Dewey notes, "all thinking is original in a projection of considerations which have not been previously apprehended."[47] By this, Dewey means that when a student is learning to think about something for the first time, that thinking is original, whether or not others have thought similar thoughts in the past. Education should, therefore, create the context for students to use information to build their own original understanding; they should use information to help them think. Dewey concludes that "no idea can possibly be conveyed as an idea from one person to another. When it is told, it is, to the one to whom it is told, another given fact, not an idea. The communication may stimulate the other person to realize the question for himself and think out a like idea, or it may smother his intellectual interest and suppress his dawning effort of thought. But what he directly gets cannot be an idea."[48] Information can stimulate thought, but it should not be confused with thought. Only by "wrestling with the conditions of the problem at first hand, seeking and finding his own way out, does [a student] think."[49] In that process, students learn how to convert "information" into something they know for themselves, the central process that can be defined as research.

Interestingly, Dewey defines information technology as one of the primary problematics to be considered in using information effectively in the educational process. We often conceive of information overload as a unique condition of our times, but Dewey notes that "the invention of appliances for securing acquaintance with remote parts of the heavens and bygone events of history; the cheapening of devices, like printing for recording and distributing information—genuine and alleged—have created an immense bulk of communicated subject matter."[50] Information technology allows the production and dissemination of such high volumes of information that "it is much easier to swamp a pupil with this [information] than to work it into his direct experience."[51] As the volume of information has increased, our conception of knowledge has changed. We have come to confuse this mass of stored information with knowledge, thereby assuming that "mastering" this mass of material constitutes knowing. Dewey claims that "the most conspicuous connotation of the word knowledge for most persons to-day (sic) is just the body of facts and truths ascertained by others; the material found in the rows and rows of atlases, cyclopedias, histories, biographies, books of travel, scientific treatises, on the shelves of libraries."[52] According to Dewey, "the imposing stupendous bulk of this material has influenced men's notions of the nature of knowledge itself." Dewey cautions us against thinking that "the record of knowledge, independent of its place as an outcome of inquiry and a resource in further inquiry, is [itself] knowledge."[53] For educational purposes, knowledge must be built incrementally in the mind of the student. "Knowledge which is mainly second-hand knowledge," Dewey claims, "tends to become merely verbal," by which he means that when knowledge is simply told to the learner, it "cannot be organized into the existing experience of the learner, it becomes mere words."[54] Knowledge is built in the learner through a process of integration and connection with what is already known.

Conclusion

Dewey's *Democracy and Education* is a tour de force of a text, a powerful statement that lays out a comprehensive rationale for progressive public education. Ranging from the complexities of advanced philosophy to the daily minutiae of classroom management, Dewey's thinking about education and its role in shaping an engaged citizenry is both profound and accessible to the average reader. For those interested specifically in information literacy, Dewey's value lies in helping us think about how this concept functions more broadly in the aims and goals of education. Dewey's vision of student learning is holistic. He envisions students learning in "authentic" contexts with problems they share with each other and care about solving. He resists academic classifications and "dualisms" that create compartmentalized knowledge, favoring, instead, a vision of the whole student at the center of, and providing coherence for, the educational process. He resists dichotomies such as student/teacher, mind/body, school/life, work/leisure. He finds the dividing of knowledge into academic subjects to be dispensed through the curriculum to be educationally dangerous. For Dewey, the student is the "site" of education, the place where learning happens. All questions of educational efficacy must therefore be resolved at the level of student growth and development. Dewey's philosophy of education begins and ends with the importance of each student's engagement in his or her own educational processes.

Much of what instruction librarians and their faculty colleagues have referred to as "active learning," "collaborative learning," "inquiry-based learning," "evidence-based learning," and "resource-based learning" owe their origins, at least in part, to Dewey's influence. Each of these efforts has focused on locating the student as the site of learning and on ways of structuring experience for students to create an authentic context for learning. As an educational reform movement, information literacy has its roots in Dewey's progressive education and the idea that democracy requires educated citizens as the heart of the democratic ideal. The current attempt of information literacy practitioners to link their agenda with service learning, authentic assessment, and student engagement, broadly conceived, is fully consistent with the pedagogies of engagement articulated in Dewey's philosophy. Perhaps the most important contribution *Democracy and Education* might make to the information literacy movement is in helping information literacy educators to think more broadly about how they can participate in these experiments in educational reform and about how they can share the overarching vision of education as a key means for creating a better society for ourselves and future generations.

Notes

1. John Dewey, *Democracy and Education: An Introduction to the Philosophy of Education* (New York: The Free Press, 1997), 89.
2. Ibid., 88.
3. Ibid., 92.
4. Ibid., 93.
5. Ibid.
6. Ibid.
7. Ibid., 94.
8. Ibid.
9. Ibid.
10. Ibid., 95.
11. Ibid.
12. Ibid., 97.
13. Ibid.
14. Ibid., 87.
15. Ibid., 119.
16. Ibid., 120–21.
17. Ibid., 20.
18. Ibid., 21.
19. Ibid., 314.

20. Ibid., 309.
21. Ibid., 306.
22. Ibid., 312–13.
23. Ibid., 310.
24. Ibid., 311.
25. Ibid., 310.
26. Ibid., 51.
27. Ibid.
28. Ibid., 56.
29. Ibid., 76.
30. Ibid., 78.
31. Ibid., 69.
32. Ibid., 70.
33. Ibid., 71.
34. Ibid., 67.
35. Ibid., 86.
36. Ibid., 86–87.
37. Ibid., 86.
38. Ibid., 158.
39. Ibid.
40. Ibid.
41. Ibid.
42. Ibid.
43. Ibid., 186.
44. Ibid.
45. Ibid., 153.
46. Ibid., 158.
47. Ibid., 159.
48. Ibid., 160.
49. Ibid.
50. Ibid., 186.
51. Ibid.
52. Ibid., 187.
53. Ibid.
54. Ibid., 188.

Librarians Enhancing Student Engagement: Partners in Learning That Build Bridges

Adrianna Kezar

"Since we started using the national survey of student engagement, librarians' role in the learning mission of our campus has become much more visible. Our skills in information literacy have become particularly important." (Librarian)

"Librarians on our campus are considered faculty and seen as influential to creating student engagement in learning." (Faculty member)

"Librarians are one of the few groups who work with people across campus in each department and division. This provides us a special vantage point in helping to create student engagement. We help build bridges between different groups that create a more coherent approach to engagement and learning." (Librarian)

"The librarians at our school make a difference in how students approach learning. Faculty make sure that students go to the library and get trained in their first year. And they also reinforce that we need to go back each year and fine tune skills. I know that I approach my studies differently than friends I have another campuses because of this involvement." (Student)

"Librarians on our campus have been instrumental in helping interpret NSSE data. They are perceived by students, faculty, and the administration as a neutral group not tied to a particular agenda." (Faculty member)

These quotes from individuals who participated in two national studies epitomize the importance of librarians in student engagement. The first study, Documenting Effective Educational Practices (DEEP), examined twenty college campuses that have exemplary levels of student engagement in order to understand what contributed to the high levels. The second study used focus groups in different regions of the country to understand the role of various groups (faculty developers, administrators, etc.) in utilizing the National Survey of Student Engagement (NSSE). Specific focus groups examined the role librarians play in implementing and interpreting the results of the NSSE. Three key themes were identified in these two research studies and are the focus of this chapter. First, the studies demonstrate that librarians play a pivotal role in creating greater student engagement. Librarians were particularly important to increasing academic challenge, enhancing active and collaborative learning, and building a supportive campus environment—three core elements of engagement as measured by NSSE. They are most successful with this effort when they partner with faculty and academic departments and help to redesign curriculum. Although librarians play a key role in student engagement, the literature and research has not highlighted this important role and this information is not widely known. The two studies described in this chapter identify this contribution and by writing about this trend, I hope to make this role more visible in the higher education community. The second key finding of this study is that librarians play a unique and important role that almost no other member of campus can play—that of bridging and integrating various groups/practices into a coherent and comprehensive network of student engagement. Third, librarians can use

NSSE data to demonstrate the importance of information literacy and its connection to student engagement, building a more central role for this aspect of learning. Before describing these three themes, it is important to have a brief introduction to the concept of student engagement and to the two studies from which the information for this chapter is drawn.

Student Engagement

In the 1990s, George Kuh began discussing and elaborating on the notion of *student engagement*. Kuh was drawing on research on student involvement from the previous thirty years and the Seven Principles of Good Practice in Undergraduate Education, which states "that level of academic challenge, time on task, and participating in other educationally purposeful activities directly influence the quality of student learning and their overall educational experience."[1] In 1998, after a decade of continued dialogue about the importance of revising undergraduate teaching and learning practices (in addition to several national reports critiquing higher education), the NSSE survey was developed to provide a tool for campuses to understand their performance and a mechanism for creating change.[2] The five NSSE benchmarks are: academic challenge, faculty student interaction, collaborative and active learning, enriching educational experiences, and a supportive campus environment.

Since the survey's inception in the late 1990s, it has become one of the most frequently used surveys in higher education. More than 750 colleges and universities have participated in it. Because it is so widely used, colleges and universities are able to examine their results and to make accurate assessments of ways to make interventions on their campuses. The NSSE initiative is aimed to further institutions' efforts to develop a culture of evidence to inform campus dialogues and action about the quality of undergraduate education.

To better understand the concept of student engagement, it is important to review the benchmarks themselves in more detail. *Level of academic challenge* refers to the importance of academic effort and setting high expectations for student performance. Examples include preparation for class, number of assigned textbooks, number of written papers or reports more than twenty pages, and coursework emphasizing synthesizing and organizing ideas, information, and experiences. *Student interaction with faculty members* is the amount and quality of time spent by students in and out of the classroom with faculty. The result is usually that faculty become role models, mentors, and guides for continuous, lifelong learning. This benchmark includes items such as discussing career plans with a faculty member or advisor, discussing ideas from a reading or class with faculty members outside class, or receiving prompt feedback from faculty on academic performance. The next benchmark is *active and collaborative learning*, in which students learn more because they are intensely involved in their education and are asked to think about and apply what they are learning in different settings. Activities that represent active and collaborative learning are: making a class presentation, working with other students on projects during class, tutoring or having taught other students, or participating in a community-based project. *Enriching educational experiences* refers to the complementary learning opportunities inside and outside classrooms that augment the academic program. Internships, capstone classes, and use of technology are examples of this benchmark. Sample questions from the survey include talking to students with different religious beliefs, political opinions, or values; and using technology to discuss or complete and assignment. *Supportive campus environment* relates to research that students perform better and are more satisfied at colleges committed to their success and cultivate positive working and social relations among different groups on campus. Examples include quality of relationship with other students, campus environment helping students cope with their nonacademic responsibilities, and quality of relationship with administrative personnel and offices.

Over the past seven years, many research studies have been conducted using NSSE data to examine trends within particular institutional types such as liberal arts colleges or to examine the national picture of how engaged students are in their learning. In addition to examining trends, individual campuses have used the data to try to understand engagement levels with their own students and to develop interventions to improve their performance. Although the survey helps to understand engagement levels, it does not help institutions to understand what produces or promotes student engagement. As a result, two studies emerged in 2002 to try to understand what promotes student engagement, in particular with high performing campuses.

Two Studies: DEEP and NSSE Roundtables

In an effort to better understand how campuses can create student engagement, the Documenting Effective Educational Practices (DEEP) project emerged. This chapter draws from the DEEP research project conducted in 2002 and 2003 by the NSSE Institute for Effective Educational Practice in partnership with the American Association of Higher Education (AAHE), with support from the Lumina Foundation. This multisite case study of twenty institutions focused on describing practices and policies that institutions have developed related to student engagement. Case study methodology allowed the twenty-four-member research team to explore the various aspects of the campus environment in depth and identify distinctive programs, practices, and policies that account for better-than-predicted levels of student engagement and graduation. The institutions selected represent the diversity of American higher education institutions—public and private, varying enrollment sizes, different missions, and varying student demographics.

Research teams (typically 3 to 5 people) conducted multiple-day visits and used several different data collection techniques: document analysis, interviews, focus groups, and observation. In total, more than 2,300 people were interviewed, many of them more than once, in an effort to learn what these schools do to promote student success. Some of the main findings from the study include a set of properties and conditions related to educationally effective colleges: a living mission and lived educational philosophy; an unshakable focus on student learning; environment adapted for educational enrichment; clear pathways to student success; an improvement-oriented ethos; and a shared responsibility for educational quality and student success.[3] The study resulted in a book and several articles for creating student engagement. The book also identifies in detail effective practices related to the five benchmarks, such as rigorous culminating experience for seniors, learning communities, undergraduate research, electronic portfolios, internships and experiential learning, peer support, and transition programs.[4] The NSSE roundtables study was conducted again in 2002–2003 by the NSSE Institute for Effective Educational Practice in partnership with AAHE. A series of focus groups was conducted in several regions of the country with groups ranging from faculty developers, librarians, student affairs administrators, academic affairs administrators, and state policymakers. Each focus group involved individuals from a range of institutions across the country and focused on understanding institutional uses of the national survey of student engagement data. Specific questions examined: impact or effect of the use of NSSE data, how participants use the data to meet their mission, how participants can interpret NSSE data for various campus constituents, and applications of the data that participants have not yet made but would like to make. The focus groups resulted in a series of policy papers entitled the National Roundtable series. (See NSSE Web site http://www.indiana.edu/~nsse/ and for the papers, http://webdb.iu.edu/Nsse/?view=deep/roundtable.) The focus group proceedings related to librarians is entitled *The Role of Integrator: Potential Opportunities for Librarians to Connect NSSE to Institutional Improvement.* In both studies, librarians emerged as pivotal players in creating student engagement. These findings are elaborated on for the remainder of the paper.

Making Visible the Role of Librarians in Learning and Student Engagement
This section highlights the way that librarians play a central role in creating student engagement. It also describes how NSSE helps to make this role more visible to college administrators so they can capitalize on this important function. The section also includes suggested ways that librarians can strategically use the survey data to capture their contribution to this role on college campuses. The key finding in the DEEP study is that educators are everywhere on campus and librarians know a good deal about how students spend their time, what they think and talk about, and how they feel, yet they are an underused educational resource. There are six themes: being recognized as part of the instructional fabric of engagement, enhancing academic challenge, increasing active and collaborative learning, creating a supportive campus environment, building faculty–librarian partnerships to support engagement, and promoting course and curriculum redesign.

Being Recognized as Part of the Instructional Fabric of Engagement
On campuses with higher-than-predicted engagement levels, librarians were integrally involved in formal aspects of the curriculum such as first-year seminars, course-related instruction, training of faculty in the disciplines and valued for their role as part of the teaching cadre. NSSE provides the potential for having the library be seen as part of the instructional fabric and can be used for increasing this role. One librarian commented about the success of using NSSE to make librarians be seen as central to learning, a role that is a challenge on many campuses: "Through our NSSE results and other surveys we are conducting, we were able to demonstrate a 15 percent improvement in retention in the past five years. We still have an even higher goal to reach. The first-year experience courses that the librarians teach have been instrumental in these efforts and highlighted our role in teaching." By demonstrating this kind of success, librarians are able to build and enhance their responsibility as part of the formal curriculum and pedagogy.

NSSE and DEEP data specifically examine librarians' roles in various aspects of campus life such as teaching first-year seminar courses or involvement in formal campuses programs. For example, DEEP schools had systematic involvement of librarians in learning from the first year to the senior year. Librarians are being used in first-year courses teaching students about research approaches and providing individual assistance. In addition to being part of first-year seminars, in the sophomore and junior years, faculty also are requiring students to take certain workshops at the library and visit the library for particular research instruction. Lastly, librarians work with students to help them develop research questions for their capstone courses. In the focus groups, librarians noted that the survey was instrumental in helping them to make a case for their role in student engagement and learning and to measure their success and to design improvements. As one librarian stated: "having NSSE data has been instrumental in helping us to understand how well the first-year experience courses were for students." Many librarians noted that surveys that campuses conduct of libraries examine customer satisfaction and do not ascertain the role of librarians in learning.

In our focus groups, librarians indicated that the NSSE benchmarks helped them make a case not just for their generic roles and involvement in learning/engagement, but also their specific roles in several benchmarks. Three benchmarks were particularly strong: academic challenge, active and collaborative learning, and creating a supportive campus environment.

Enhancing Academic Challenge
The current generation of students has grown up in a very different environment. Because they spend time on the computer, watching television, and playing video games, their strategies and approaches to learning are distinctive. Many faculty struggle to understand how to engage students who come out of this environment. Librarians' emphasis on information literacy fits well with the autonomous and technology-oriented style of these learners. When we spoke to students on campuses with high levels of student engagement, they describe their interest in problem-based learning that stemmed from their own interests. They said that what excited them most about college was the ability to conduct their own research and that learning the skills of accessing information resources, using technology tools effectively, and understanding how information is situated and produced helped create the kind of academic challenge they hoped for and expected from college. Students noted that

the library was an area where they found these skills were developed, and for some students this was their primary source of academic challenge. Some campuses were quite intentional in the way they formed partnerships between departments/units and librarians working together in teams to create more challenging courses and curriculum. Another example of the way that librarians enhance academic challenge was described by a librarian: "library staff work closely with students in their first-year seminar and capstone projects. We help them to develop research questions and conduct research. We also archive the projects because this encourages seriousness toward the work among all students. We see students striving harder because they know this work is public."

Increasing Active and Collaborative Learning
The library is a site where learning is often active through the use of technology. Today's student is a savvy technology user and tends to define active learning in terms of technology. This is the area where faculty generally feel less comfortable. Librarians are highly trained in technology usage and can make an important contribution to active and collaborative learning on campuses. Also, many faculty prefer the lecture approach. As one student noted: "I get bored in the classroom; sometimes faculty are just lecturing at me. What I get really excited about is doing research, and I found the library a great location for looking at archives, learning about key information sites on the Internet, and searching specialized databases." Librarians have been trained in more active pedagogies and they can be models of this type of teaching on campus. The faculty development staff member commented on how they have librarians give brown bags on a regular basis on information literacy and active learning techniques.

Creating a Supportive Campus Environment
Another area where they saw their contribution to learning was in the area of creating a supportive campus environment. Most libraries offer a host of support services that are critical for student success in their coursework from research training to technology support to time management courses. Engaged students noted how they commonly interacted with library staff and resources. Repeatedly, students on "high-engagement" campuses told us that the library created a space where they wanted to participate in learning. Many of the campuses we visited had innovative libraries with social space,

restaurants and coffee shops, and amenable meeting rooms. These campuses tried to create distinctive architecture where tables and chairs could be moved so that students could work in groups together to foster a collaborative learning environment. Therefore, support was created through services offered, but also through the architecture and physical environment that made students feel invited into the space and interested in engaging further with other students in learning. This trend reflects the "learning commons" movement in space planning/library renovation in which design emphasizes bringing together the social and academic lives of students.

Building Faculty–Librarian Partnerships to Support Engagement

One key way that librarians noted they work to create engagement was through partnerships with faculty and departments. In our national focus groups, most librarians described their struggle to get faculty engaged in discussions about learning and the way the library can support faculty work. One librarian described a story illustrating this disconnect between faculty and librarians:

> A faculty member came to complain to me that the students in their [his] course only used Internet resources and he wanted them to search specialized databases and use books and articles. I told him that he could design the assignment so that using only Internet sources would not be appropriate. These are the things that often do not occur to faculty.

The literature in higher education often describes the way faculty prefer to work autonomously, are bound within disciplinary silos, and do not work collaboratively with other academic staff.[5] This literature identifies a persistent challenge for creating these types of meaningful partnerships that support student engagement. Several recent publications have tried to emphasize the importance of faculty working in collaboration with other academic staff. (See *Powerful Partnerships: A Shared Responsibility for Learning*, National Association for Student Personnel Administrators and the American Association for Higher Education, 1998.)

Other librarians commented on the disconnect between faculty and librarians and its impact on students becoming information literate. In the words of another, "Our students are getting farther and farther behind in understanding information, but there are limited ways for us to connect with faculty to bridge this growing gap." However, NSSE data were seen as a potential resource for bringing faculty and librarians together. The definition of learning in NSSE is broad and the benchmarks cross many areas of campus. It forces people to think outside the classroom for sources of learning and has the potential for having faculty think more consciously about other partners in the learning process.

Also, the NSSE results can be used to understand whether faculty are partnering with librarians and prioritizing information literacy. NSSE identifies whether faculty are engaging students in discussions about the use and importance of the library for their academic development. Other questions explore whether students are engaging with library resources.

Our research on campuses that have high student engagement demonstrated that librarians were seen as partners with faculty. This was manifested in many different forms. On smaller campuses, individual faculty members have developed relationships with librarians and partner to integrate the librarians into key parts of their courses and curriculum. On larger campuses, schools and colleges have developed structured relationships (with set activities to integrate librarians in courses and include orientation of faculty, for example) with the librarians and communicate at key points throughout the year. What is evident on these highly engaged campuses is that faculty recognize the importance of students' becoming information literate and the impact of this development process on their learning. As a result, librarians are brought into classes, workshops, and orientations on a regular basis. Librarians are integrated into faculty development programs at these highly engaged campuses; such integration helps faculty realize the need for students to use the library resources and training. In the words of one student: "I feel much more confident doing my assignments because of the workshops I have taken. I'm really glad that the faculty encouraged us to take the workshop and it has resulted in me using many more resources than I have in the past."

Promoting Course and Curriculum Redesign
An important use of NSSE data for creating student engagement was rethinking course design. One librarian described the way she used NSSE for this purpose: "Occasionally, faculty come to the library with questions. NSSE provides us with data for helping faculty to redesign assignments or library

training sessions. It also provides us with ideas for outreach to faculty." Using NSSE results, librarians can design a workshop on how to raise the academic challenge of course assignments. As one person stated: "I can now discuss how academic challenge is seen as low on campus and provide techniques for making an assignment more challenging through the types of research students conduct and the resources they are asked to use. Before, I would not have had these specific types of ideas for improvement. With NSSE, I can make these specific recommendations for course redesign and truly become a partner with faculty in the learning process." This example also demonstrates the way that librarians helped to foster academic challenge. Data also provided librarians with evidence that they could pass on to faculty and academic departments about information literacy that would help individuals and units understand the need for course redesign and for involving librarians in that process.

Helping to Create a Comprehensive Approach to Student Engagement
In the national focus group study, we discovered that librarians were generally not integrated into the information dissemination process of NSSE data or plans for developing greater student engagement. Although librarians are familiar with ways to display and interpret data for multiple constituents, campuses have been slow to see their role in the use and interpretation of NSSE data. A key discovery at the roundtables was that librarians are an untapped source of support and interpretation. However, on the "high-engagement" campuses we studied, librarians were key players in interpreting the NSSE survey data and were seen as agents of student engagement. The range of ways that librarians can use NSSE data for campus improvement was striking and suggests that campuses should involve librarians as they move forward with planning efforts focused on curricular expansion or revision. In addition, they can play a bridging role that few on campus are prepared to play, helping to create a campuswide plan. In the following section, I want to encourage more campuses to involve librarians in the interpretation and implementation of NSSE survey and in designing plans for student engagement.

A Neutral Source for Interpretation of Data
Because librarians tend to be seen as neutral parties on campus, they can be reliable interpreters of the NSSE data, especially as related to poor or disputed results. Librarians are seen as having fewer agendas and being more open to multiple perspectives; also, the library is a place where all faculty, students,

and staff come and mingle. One librarian described the integrating role of the library this way: "There are no divisions at the library. People do not see themselves at the library as in the sciences or humanities or in academic or student affairs. They come here as researchers and learners." One campus story helped to demonstrate the important role librarians can play in data interpretation:

> We conducted the NSSE student survey as well as a comparative report of faculty and their impressions of the learning environment. The results between the students and faculty are quite different. Students feel the campus is less rigorous than faculty. The General Education Committee is going to take up the issue. However, most faculty want to disregard the student data. Also, the institutional research office is seen on many campuses as an instrument of the administration. Therefore, the institutional research office's interpretation of the NSSE results are seen as laden with administrative values or priorities. Librarians, however, are not seen as vested or tied to any interest group. Therefore, we can help to create discussions around the data that no other group on campus can develop.

The perception that librarians are neutral interpreters and have a lack of investment in individual agendas was seen as a great resource for helping to create an environment where data are used for campus improvement.

Using Their Role on Campus Teams and Networks to Create Change

In addition to being seen as neutral interpreters, librarians are often asked to serve on campuswide committees developed to examine specific issues such as general education or problems on campus such as retention. Because librarians are often assigned to such teams, they can use their special status as neutral interpreter to have people examine the NSSE data in nondefensive ways. Campus teams are only one venue in which librarians have contact with people across campus. Each librarian is assigned to a set of departments or divisions. Through these assignments, they interact with faculty and staff across campus. This cross-boundary work can be instrumental in helping to interpret NSSE data and for institutional improvement. As one librarian commented: "We talk to people across campus in ways that most other employees do not. This provides us a special vantage point for using NSSE data to enhance the performance." This helps move planning for engagement from a unit or division into a campuswide activity. Campuses that had high levels of student engagement recognized the special role of the librarians in fostering communications among groups across campus, and they intentionally and consciously placed librarians on key committees to ensure success of campuswide efforts.

Increasing Academic Rigor and Focusing on Outcomes Campuswide

On today's campuses, academic rigor and documenting student outcomes are common concerns that present particular challenges, especially as they need to be engaged by the entire campus. Increasingly, accreditation agencies are focusing on outcomes assessment and campuses will no longer be able to avoid these cross-campus planning issues. However, this kind of assessment is a contentious issue because various groups across campus look at the outcomes in very different ways. For example, in the sciences, faculty are often able to identify discrete competencies whereas in the humanities they may be less likely to identify such discrete outcomes. One librarian commented: "We have had regional-, discipline-, and profession-specific accreditation visits. Each visit provided the same message to our campus: we needed to think of ways to improve the student learning experience and document student outcomes. I now see that I can use NSSE to work with other employees on campus to achieve this goal. Librarians are seen as key sources for interpreting data on our campus and one that is not invested with any particular ideology." This librarian, like others, sees that NSSE data are being used to help resolve problems identified by external groups and stakeholders.

Being a Repository and Communicator for NSSE Data

Campuses with high levels of student engagement use the library as a repository for NSSE results. Some campuses have NSSE results posted on their Web sites, but it might be password protected, allowing only limited access. Others post only partial NSSE results so that people are not overwhelmed or only publish the positive results. However it is done, it is important to have a central location where information can be kept over time. The library plays the key role on these campuses as a neutral location for keeping this important information that helps with campus decision making. These campuses also called on librarians to present NSSE data to key communities. According to one faculty member: "We have created a team with our institutional research office and librarians. These teams go around to various meetings that make decisions related to teaching and learning and present data to help us inform our decision making."

Bringing Greater Attention to the Connection between Information Literacy and Student Engagement

The last major theme that emerged in the research is the way that highly engaged campuses included information literacy as a part of the student engagement movement. Faculty, staff, and students recognized the special skill of librarians in teaching people to "learn how to learn." Librarians described the ways they can use NSSE data to make the link between information literacy and student engagement (seeing information literacy as an active form of learning) and increasing academic challenge. Administrators worked to support librarians and create a shared vision across campus of the importance information literacy.

Recognizing Information Literacy as Engagement

Various individuals at institutions that have a high level of student engagement noted that notions of learning are changing to focus on information literacy and that the NSSE data are pivotal in helping make this transition. Academic engagement is increasingly being defined as information literacy and campuses need to be more aware of framing engagement and academic challenge in this way. Librarians are a great source for understanding this type of engagement and have some understanding about the level of information literacy among students on campus based on their day-to-day work. One administrator commented about the library's importance in shaping engagement efforts: "increasingly on our campus the discussion has changed from thinking mostly about process, such as creating more experiential or collaborative learning, to more thought on the substance around areas we are trying to create engagement. As we move more towards this issue of the substance, information literacy has become a goal we are striving for. As we made this recognition about the importance of information literacy to our students, we also realize the importance of more intentionally including librarians as part of our learning team."

Measuring the Extent of Information Literacy

Two benchmarks were seen as critical for measuring information literacy: active and collaborative learning and academic challenge. The survey questions related to type of assignments helped to determine whether students are expected to be consumers and critical analysts of information. NSSE has provided a tool for librarians to demonstrate to campus officials that low levels of information literacy exist and to develop strategic plans for enhancing this outcome among students. Data are critical in order to make information literacy a strategic priority within campus operations. NSSE's high response rate makes it a credible source to use in making arguments for the need to increase resources for information literacy efforts. Librarians can use NSSE data to support a new learning environment focused on information literacy. By obtaining NSSE results, librarians can use data to develop a collective understanding of information literacy on their campuses; further, they can develop a set of explanatory data accompanying the primary data that can be distributed in order to shape decision making about curriculum revision. One librarian noted: "I bring the NSSE survey results to every meeting that I go to. I never know when I might have an opportunity to make the case for the need to improve information literacy on our campus."

Supporting and Creating a Shared Vision of Information Literacy

On campuses with high levels of student engagement, administrators described the way they supported librarians in their efforts to teach students to "learn how to learn." Many of these administrators have now included information literacy as part of their strategic planning or educational reform efforts. Most senior administrators are reexamining undergraduate education, focusing on innovations such as service learning, undergraduate research, collaborative learning, and first-year interest groups. Moreover, information literacy is emerging as another reform movement that leads to student engagement. Discussing information literacy in conjunction with these other reforms, and as a part of general strategic planning about learning for the campus, is one of the successful strategies of campuses with high engagement levels. Having established a shared vision, faculty, staff, and administrators have noted that they see more collaboration around these educational innovations, including information literacy.

Many administrators noted that planning efforts need to be combined with substantive changes in how staff work. The vision provides a starting place for making alterations, oftentimes major changes, in the way that roles and responsibilities are enacted, priorities developed, and rewards allocated. For librarians, this may mean moving from one-time seminars or workshops on information literacy to working more closely with faculty in general education reform, for example. One-time workshops are unlikely to create institutionalized change around information literacy. One librarian commented on her campus's efforts to rethink the work of librarians: "as many people have mentioned here today in this focus group, becoming more integrated into the institutional fabric of learning means that we need to conduct our work differently. Many campuses talk about this aspirationally but are not making necessary changes in roles and responsibilities. Often additional committees or work get added to librarians' workload rather than rethinking roles, and people are confused about priorities. We have been actively examining responsibilities and whether we really need to do some of the work that we are currently doing rather than simply adding on more and more responsibilities so that people can focus their work in the most productive and fruitful areas."

Conclusion

Librarians find themselves at a particularly opportune time. Tools such as the National Survey of Student Engagement can be used to help demonstrate librarians' pivotal roles in the learning environment. NSSE data provide a very persuasive argument for including librarians in more substantive ways in academic planning and in the institutional fabric of teaching and learning. They also provide support for librarians' efforts to support information literacy as an educational innovation.

Notes

1. George Kuh, "Assessing What Really Matters to Student Learning: Inside the National Survey of Student Engagement," *Change* (May/June 2001): 12.

2. ———, "How Are We Doing at Engaging Students?" *About Campus* (Mar.–Apr. 2003): 9–16.

3. G. Kuh, J. Kinzie, J.Schuh, and E. Whitt & Associates, *Student Success in College: Creating Conditions That Matter* (San Francisco: Jossey-Bass, 2005).

4. Ibid.

5. A. Kezar, "Achieving Student Success: Strategies for Creating Partnerships between Academic and Student Affairs," *NASPA Journal* 41, no. 1 (2003): 1–22;

————, "Moving from I to We: Re-organizing for Collaboration in Higher Education," *Change: The Magazine of Higher Learning* (July/Aug. 2005): 42–52.

Bibliography

Kezar, A., "Achieving Student Success: Strategies for Creating Partnerships between Academic and Student Affairs, *NASPA Journal* 41, no. 1 (2003): 1–22.

Kezar, A., "Moving from I to We: Re-organizing for Collaboration in Higher Education, *Change: The Magazine of Higher Learning* (July/Aug. 2005): 42–52.

Kuh, G., J. Kinzie, J. Schuh, and E. Whitt & Associates, *Student Success in College: Creating Conditions That Matter* (San Francisco: Jossey-Bass, 2005).

Kuh, G., "How Are We Doing at Engaging Students?" *About Campus* (Mar.–Apr. 2003): 9–16.

Kuh, G., "Assessing What Really Matters to Student Learning: Inside the National Survey of Student Engagement, *Change* (May/June 2001): 10–18.

Becoming Educated: Service Learning as Mirror

Margit Watts

Through others, we become ourselves.

L. S. Vygotsky

This chapter focuses on the pedagogies that guide our institutions of higher learning, the challenges we encounter across the nation, and some of the opportunities we have to engage our students more fully in their educational experience. By looking at the prevailing research on student engagement, one finds that a return to experiential education is a hot topic of discussion and the integration of service learning is beginning to be viewed as an excellent mechanism through which such learning takes place. For the past fourteen years, the University of Hawaii at Manoa has offered freshmen a learning community opportunity in the form of the Rainbow Advantage Program. Students who enrolled in this program took many of their first-year credits together, but most important, they participated in weekly service learning activities to augment their classroom learning. The service learning projects took many forms over the years, but all contributed in numerous ways to the development of academic skills, many of them closely associated with what we call information literacy skills. This chapter gives an overview of the philosophies behind this kind of learning and offers examples of the various service learning projects and how they relate closely to the kinds of skills with which we hope students will graduate.

The Purpose of a Liberal Education

As Mark Edmundson aptly stated in his book, *Why Read?*, the questions that lie at the core of a liberal education are:

- Who am I?
- What might I become?
- What is this world in which I find myself?
- How might it be changed for the better?[1]

Do students today view the buffet of liberal arts curricula we offer as a way to answer these questions? Do they understand that our general education requirements are actually based on decades of discourse about what makes an educated person? Do they have any notion of the concept of education for democracy? And maybe the more important question is, Do those of us working in institutions of higher learning offer anything to help them understand? Throughout his or her experience in higher education, a student is guided to explore many different content areas, each discipline offering unique information and perspectives. The most important outcome is the development of an educated person, a thinking and productive citizen of the community.

Though students seem to view higher education as a pipeline to a better future (read career), the fact is that in our present-day economics, we are not automatically offering the American Dream to each student who earns a college degree. Arthur Levine and Jeanette S. Cureton captured the angst of students well in their book, *When Hope and Fear Collide*, suggesting that students want to hope for the future while still being afraid that when they graduate, the world will not be awaiting their arrival with open arms (or great paying jobs).[2]

> *It can only be because of the conviction that something in the undergraduate experience will lead to a more competent, more concerned, more complete human being.*
>
> *Ernest Boyer*

A liberal arts education is about attaining knowledge, wisdom, and understanding. It is supposed to promote inquiry, interaction, and collaboration. It is meant to be transformative, reflective, and integrative. Above all, it is eventually supposed to help students make sense of their lives. Given all these goals, what should we offer to help students embrace the concept that a college education will help them become this "complete human being?" How can we expect students to appreciate the process rather than be focused on the product when we do not teach in a connected manner? Most often, students experience a liberal education within the construct of a fragmented curriculum. They are checking off courses on a worksheet, which requires them to take three courses in social sciences, two in languages, three in humanities, and so forth. They know they are to complete some collection of general education courses that cross multiple disciplines, but they are not necessarily convinced what these courses will do for them in the long run. Moreover, most institutions do not make connections across all these foundational courses to help students make meaning of them outside the confines of the classroom.

Additionally, there is great distance between faculty and students, especially with the prevailing pedagogy of lecture and routine testing. Students often go through college without making a close connection to any faculty member as mentor. Finally, the teaching of theory without regard to practice often promotes an educational culture that reinforces passivity and ultimately leads to high rates of student attrition. In many respects, our institutions of higher learning mirror our larger society—fragmented and alienated. No wonder students are fearful for their futures.

Engaging Students

In *The End of Education*, Neil Postman argued that we no longer have a "narrative" to serve as a foundation that helps us answer the question of *why* we should be educated. He suggested that we have spoken far too much about what and how to educate and noted that educators have spent the past twenty years speculating on how we might best teach a content area, what the optimum class size might be, how much traditional literature should be included, whether team teaching is a good approach, whether active learning should be a component in all classrooms, and other pedagogical considerations. Postman suggested, however, that educators have not, in fact, addressed the question of *why* education at all.[3]

Moreover, the report of the Wingspread Group on Higher Education, *An American Imperative*, suggests that there are at least three issues of consequence to all universities across the nation, regardless of the diversity found among them. These fundamental issues are: (1) taking values seriously, (2) putting student learning first, and (3) creating a nation of learners.[4] Students are indeed asking "why" education and universities are slowly trying to answer with innovative programs, new teaching and learning strategies, and new approaches to the issues of retention and engagement. No matter what discipline, how large the university, or which perspective might create our palette of educational expectations, we are all challenged to develop teaching and learning environments that not only will retain students, but also will engage them and open their minds to the intellectual inquiry at the core of a higher education.

A passion for learning is not something we should need to inspire in our students; rather, it is what we must keep from being extinguished. The challenge faced by colleges and universities nationwide is one of a lack of engagement by students in their education. This leads to problems with retention and graduation rates, not to mention the loss of intellectual curiosity that could lead to a less informed citizenry. George D. Kuh, in the most recent National Survey of Student Engagement (NSSE), reports that what students do during college counts more in terms of desired outcomes than who they are or even where they go to college. His research on college student development illustrates that the time and energy students devote to educationally purposeful activities is the single best predictor of their learning and personal development.[5]

Human beings are by nature passionate, curious, and intrigued, and will seek to connect, find patterns, and make sense of things. Learning is more effective when new information is made meaningful and linked to personal experience or prior knowledge; when we learn how to evaluate, assess, and connect, information is transformed into knowledge. Unfortunately, most undergraduates experience higher education in the traditional manner, which does not often include direct involvement in the creation of knowledge.

> *Service helps people realize their own limitations*
> *Walter Clark (first-year student)*

In its 1998 report, "Reinventing Undergraduate Education," the Boyer Commission recommended that students be given opportunities to learn through inquiry and that research-based learning become the standard. The report states that "the experience of most undergraduates at most research universities is that of receiving what is served out to them."[6] It further suggests that the ideal would be to turn the "prevailing undergraduate culture of receivers into a culture of inquirers, a culture in which faculty, graduate students, and undergraduates share an adventure of discovery." The engagement of undergraduates in research and creative scholarship and the provision of applied educational experiences, including service learning, are important imperatives for the future of higher education. Students regularly miss the relationship between the information-seeking process and the actual creation of knowledge. An institution of higher education is a place where knowledge is kept, created, revised, organized, manipulated, bantered about, reformed, added to, constructed, deconstructed, and reconstructed. Most students are not allowed to view how all this fits together and what role they themselves might play. Ultimately, the goal of infusing the undergraduate curriculum with research-based learning is to facilitate students' ability to define the meaning of research for themselves. The NSSE report endorses the movement toward engaging students more fully in a variety of activities that help them understand scholarship—the creation of knowledge.

If one major goal of higher education is to create lifelong learners, what we have to offer them should meet that challenge. We need students to be engaged in their educational process so that they take away an appreciation of learning that will sustain them throughout their lives. According to William James, reality is pure experience and on the basis of our experience we construct a theory of reality. This is what we should aspire to as we educate our students.

Experiential Learning

> *Learning is no more than a sector of cognitive development that is facilitated by experience.*
>
> Jean Piaget

An abyss has grown between our pedagogies and our experience. In an effort to restructure teaching and learning, many institutions have begun to address the challenge of engaging students by designing a curriculum that students find significant, often referred to as experiential education. One of the "Seven Principles for Good Teaching" in undergraduate education is the encouragement of active learning, and to emphasize this, Arthur Chickering states: "learning is not a spectator sport."[7] Howard Radest suggests that our community of scholars is so often behind the closed doors of the classroom that the real community disappears. He views the failure of becoming a community of scholars as one more instance of lost connections.[8]

> *One way that doing service learning makes you a better*
> *person is that it makes you aware of who you really are;*
> *you become tolerant and open-minded.*
>   *Travis Chang (first-year student)*

Some view experiential education as the oldest form of education—learning by doing. It is a pedagogical approach that integrates student experiences into the curriculum. It is an educational strategy that connects classroom theory with practice in the real world and is a process through which a learner constructs knowledge. Much of the theory behind experiential learning builds on the concept of the social nature of learning. Students learn in specific times and places; thus, there is a view to moral development and learning within the actual diversities in our communities. In *Habits of the Heart*, Robert Bellah suggested that "there are voices calling for a reaffirmation of the classic role of education as a way to articulate private aspirations with common cultural meanings so that individuals simultaneously become more fully developed people and citizens of a free society."[9] There are many forms of experiential learning—in class hands-on activities, internships and apprenticeships, laboratory settings, and, of course, service-learning projects, all viable approaches to engage students in their academic experiences.

Service Learning: An Overview

> *Insight, I believe, refers to that depth of understanding*
> *that comes by setting experiences, yours and mine,*
> *familiar and exotic, new and old, side by side, learning*
> *to let them speak to one another.*
>   *Mary Catherine Bateson*

In *Peripheral Vision*, Mary Catherine Bateson suggested that "by encountering and comparing more than one version of experience," we can learn that our realities and those of others are relative and dependent on both context and point of view.[10] No one will argue about the significance of getting today's youth involved in meaningful ways in their own communities. However, many disagree about how much value this kind of activity has within the construct of an academic environment. Perhaps exploring the possibilities of service learning as a breeding ground for both the enhancement of academic learning and a catalyst for engagement and passion could curb the disagreement.

Jacques Barzun suggested that the task of higher education is to pass on a social, cultural, and political heritage to the next generation. A well-educated person is seen as someone open to new cultures, ideas, and technologies as well as one who remains current through independent learning.[11] If one of the missions of an institution of higher education is to foster learning, discovery, discussion, and the gathering of information about the world, is it part of the academic mission of a university to change students' orientations toward their communities? There is general agreement that we want to develop thoughtful citizens who contribute time to their communities. And most of us understand that education is not a one-way affair, nor is it value free. But how much are we willing to incorporate and integrate community service into the curriculum? How, why, and in what ways do we want our students to change throughout their undergraduate years? In 1987, Ernest L. Boyer suggested that undergraduates today are "products of a society in which the call for individual gratification booms forth on every side while the claims of community are weak."[12] Perhaps we need to help students see the relationship between what they learn and how they live.

> *It made me understand the common struggles in people's lives. I had never volunteered in my life before. It made me understand and realize each person makes a difference in someone's life and future. It also made me more patient with the human race.*
> *Jonathan Aguilar (first-year student)*

The basic theory of service learning in an academic environment belongs to John Dewey, who was very clear in his understanding that the key to learning is found in the interaction of knowledge and skills with experience. The new movement of integrating community service within the curriculum is attempting to bridge the gap between theory and practice. The call for service is both a call for practical experience to enhance learning and a reinforcement of moral and civic values inherent in serving others. There is the hope that something within a student's undergraduate experience will lead to the development of a more competent and more complete human being.

> *There are a lot of things you don't know about yourself until you give back to people who need things more than you.*
>
> *(first-year RAP student)*

As service learning has become more central to the pedagogy of higher education, it has been defined in many ways. The following are a few examples of definitions by organizations closely involved in promoting this kind of experiential learning:

• Service learning is a method through which citizenship, academic subjects, skills, and values are taught. It involves active learning, drawing lessons from the experience of performing service work. *Developed by the Corporation on National and Community Service as part of their briefing materials for national community service.*

• Service-learning means a method under which students learn and develop through thoughtfully-organized service that: is conducted in and meets the needs of a community and is coordinated with an institution of higher education, and with the community; helps foster civic responsibility; is integrated into and enhances the academic curriculum of the students enrolled; and includes structured time for students to reflect on the service experience. *American Association for Higher Education (AAHE): Series on Service-Learning to the Disciplines (adapted from the National and Community Service Trust Act of 1993)*

• Service-learning is a teaching method which combines community service with academic instruction as it focuses on critical, reflective thinking and civic responsibility. Service-learning programs involve students in organized community service that addresses local needs, while developing their academic skills, sense of civic responsibility, and commitment to the community. *Community College National Center for Community Engagement*

• Service-learning is a credit-bearing, educational experience in which students participate in an organized service activity that meets identified community needs and reflects on the service activity in such a way as to gain further understanding of course content, a broader appreciation of the discipline, and an enhanced sense of civic responsibility. *Erobert Bringle and Julie Hatcher, "A Service Learning Curriculum for Faculty." The Michigan Journal of Community Service Learning. Fall 1995, 112–22.*

• Service-learning is the various pedagogies that link community service and academic study so that each strengthens the other. The basic theory of service-learning is Dewey's: the interaction of knowledge and skills with experience is key to learning. *Thomas Ehrlich, in: Barbara Jacoby and Associates. Service-Learning in Higher Education: Concepts and Practices. San Francisco, CA: Jossey-Bass, 1996.*

Service to others is an ideal that has served America well throughout history. If we are a democracy of participation, service to the community can be seen as a place to learn about the democracy we value. Service learning actually offers an enhanced and experiential opportunity to decide how to live one's life. Additionally, service learning has proven to raise self-esteem, build character, empower students to see themselves as integral players within their communities, foster the development of lifelong commitments, and give students opportunities to become responsible, engaged adults. Benefits also include a place for critical reflection, better comprehension of course content, and the integration of theory and practice. Thus, classroom instruction and community service combine synergistically to enhance learning; students begin to take ownership of their learning. Boyer writes that service learning "offers opportunities that cannot be obtained any other way. And such an experience may be one of the first truly meaningful acts in a young person's life.[13] In a research study of more than 1,500 college students, Alan S. Waterman found that students considered their service learning experience to be of higher quality than their regular classes and "that they worked harder, learned more and were more intellectually stimulated."[14]

Service learning experiences provide contexts through which students can better understand abstract coursework. Some of the benefits are:

• Connecting to the community to solve real problems: When students work with various agencies in the community, they participate in developing and/or implementing solutions to problems; the issues addressed are not theoretical but are those found in real life, which need real-life answers.

• Helping students see themselves as an integral part of the community: One of the main goals of education is to help people become productive citizens within their communities; working in service learning environments gives students experience that can be used later in their own communities.

- **Becoming aware of diversity:** When students reach out and spend time in new environments, they come face to face with diverse members of the community.
- **Reinforcing democratic values and citizenship:** The whole notion of American democracy is based on a participatory government; students begin to see that they have a duty to America as a free citizen to contribute.
- **Learning a variety of new skills:** In any new experience students pick up skills that are new; skills will vary depending on the service learning site.
- Allowing for nonacademic strengths to shine: All students bring a variety of skills, talents, and strengths to any situation; their work in a service learning environment will allow them to share some of these, be they organizational, musical, artistic, or other skills.
- **Enhancing the academic curriculum:** If students choose carefully, their experiences in service learning can give them an insight into the more theoretical work in the classroom.

The following goals are what have motivated more and more institutions of higher learning to include service learning as an integral part of their academics:

- Development of opportunities to integrate theory and practice
- Increase the understanding of social issues
- Teach students to work in teams and collaboratively
- Enhancement of critical thinking skills
- Sharpen problem-solving skills
- Strengthen a sense of social responsibility
- Provide a heightened understanding of human differences and commonalities
- Building self-confidence
- Illuminating personal values and beliefs
- Discovering a sense of empathy
- Offer time for reflecting on what is learned

Many new educational models suggest that students need to be invested in the learning process and that they do their best learning when they can apply knowledge and/or relate it to themselves. Experiences such as service learning can lead to deep and connected learning and can help students make meaning of their academic learning.

Students will gain the understanding of how to analyze methods for solving problems. The specific material covered in their courses will be broadened and their understanding of the subject matter will be deepened. Experiences such as service learning increase the complexity of learning. Most important, when students are involved in a service learning project, they are more interested in the subject matter, more motivated to succeed, and will understand more clearly the importance of academic work.

Service Learning and Information Literacy

> *Growth is very important in developing knowledge and wisdom. By growing from life experiences, you take with you the new information learned in order to conquer the next big step.*
> *Tamaryne Byrne (first-year student)*

Service learning offers an enhanced and experiential opportunity to augment academic learning. Using information literacy skills in a service learning environment offers opportunities to do problem solving in real life situations. The more we can steep higher learning in real-life experiences, the more likely we are to see students engaged in their educational process. An important learning objective is to develop information literacy skills from the perspective of the student as an end user in real-life situations. Thus, service learning can lead to "knowing" actually being personal knowledge. What better way to begin answering Who am I? in an informed manner? Pair this with the notion that today's world embodies a rapidly shrinking half-life of information, and one understands how information literacy skills can be viewed as necessary to survival. We hope to build social responsibility, abilities to assess and evaluate information both efficiently and critically, and finally to be able to use it to create knowledge both accurately and creatively. In much of his work, Dewey identified reflective thinking with problem solving. In other words, we do not think unless we have a problem to solve. The acquisition of information literacy skills is necessary to making informed decisions—to solve problems.

> *Knowledge, after all, is justified belief.*
> *Jerome Bruner*

There are multiple definitions of information literacy. However, Ilene F. Rockman offers a broad definition that serves the purpose of this narrative well. She suggests that information literacy is "a set of abilities that allow a person to recognize when information is needed and to effectively and efficiently act on that need."[15] Actually, information literacy could be viewed as a survival skill in today's information- overloaded world. Perhaps it should even be considered a social responsibility, as citizens need to be able to assess information efficiently, evaluate it critically, and then use it accurately and/or creatively. Connecting ideas, thinking critically, acting responsibly, and communicating effectively are all essential to lifelong learning and active engagement in today's world. One could determine that an important learning objective is to develop information literacy skills from the perspective of the student as an end user in real-life situations.

> *...an extended notion of information literacy is essential to the future of democracy, if citizens are to be intelligent shapers of the information society rather than its pawns.*
>
> *Jeremy Shapiro*

Patricia Senn Breivik finds that information literacy "can be a powerful tool in the linking of campuses to their communities."[16] We can combine the development of information literacy skills with service learning endeavors and offer students problem-solving situations in real-life situations. Rockman agrees with Breivik and finds that the integration of information literacy competencies into service learning programs "can have a mutually beneficial outcome to students as they learn to develop and use research skills within the real world of their communities."[17] Of course, above and beyond the benefits to lifelong learning and becoming active and knowledgeable citizens of a community, service and reflection experiences increase an understanding of course content and encourage thinking in a more complex and critical manner.

Service Learning: Guidelines

> *Information literacy is the ability to both learn and,*

perhaps more importantly, understand the information
that is given to you.
David Newstead (first-year student)

Using both Information Literacy Competency Standards for Higher Education and Characteristics for Best Practices in teaching information literacy as guidelines help illustrate the various approaches one could take in developing a program utilizing service learning to teach information literacy skills. The standards were reviewed and approved by a committee of the Association of College and Research Libraries in the hopes that all appropriate professional and accreditation associations would endorse them. The Best Practices Characteristics attempt to articulate elements of exemplary programs at both two- and four-year institutions. To frame the examples in this section, the standards and characteristics are listed below.

Competency Standards

1. The information-literate student determines the nature and extent of the information needed.
2. The information-literate student accesses needed information effectively and efficiently.
3. The information-literate student evaluates information and its sources critically and incorporates selected information into his or her knowledge base and value system.
4. The information-literate student, individually or as a member of a group, uses information effectively to accomplish a specific purpose.
5. The information-literate student understands many of the economic, legal, and social issues surrounding the use of information and accesses and uses information ethically and legally.

Characteristics of Best Practices in the Teaching of Information Literacy

1. **Mission**—make the program/course mission intersect that of your institution
2. **Goals and Objectives**—keep these clear and in line with the goals and objectives of your academic strategic plan
3. **Planning**—know the outcomes that are desirable and plan to meet them

4. **Administrative and Institutional Support**—by aligning information literacy work with the strategic plan of the institution, support will more likely be forthcoming
5. **Articulation with the Curriculum**—programs and courses should integrate with existing curriculum
6. **Collaboration**—bringing in faculty and staff from across campus
7. **Pedagogy**—initiating conversations about appropriate pedagogy
8. **Staffing**—an issue of relevance and budget
9. **Outreach**—keep everyone informed of the information literacy work
10. **Assessment/Evaluation**—have this be an integral part of both the planning and the actual implementation

Both sets of guidelines reach across many aspects of a higher education curriculum. A wide range of programs and projects can be developed that integrate, either intrinsically or extrinsically, service learning and the learning of information literacy skills. In its broadest sense, service learning is an experiential method of expanding a student's learning in whatever field or course it occurs. Thus, when seen as an extension of classroom learning, it lends itself to the acquisition of information literacy skills and competencies.

Service Learning: A Case Study
The Rainbow Advantage Program (RAP) is a tightly woven learning community based on the coordinated studies model. Students are actively engaged in their education and participate in a variety of approaches to learning. Education in this program is seen as the process of open-ended inquiry, and students are challenged to view learning as the development and building of connections. Therefore, the focus is on collaborative teaching strategies, cooperative learning techniques, a wide use of technology, and a variety of links to the wider community.

In order to produce lifelong learners, the collaborative teacher–learner model, allowing for the kind of environment that encourages the students to be creative, original thinkers, and continually analyzing and evaluating their own learning, replaces the teacher as bearer of knowledge model. Emphasis is placed on acquiring communication, critical thinking, and research skills.

Monkeys can know facts, birds can know facts, anyone can know facts, but they may not know useful facts.

*Education is useful, knowing lots of unapplied facts
is not.*

Katie Thomas (first-year student)

A liberal education helps students acquire an integrated base of knowledge, develop communication skills, enhance higher-order thinking skills, become acquainted with methods of inquiry, examine personal values and social mores, foster an awareness of other cultures, gain self-knowledge, and achieve lasting intellectual and cultural interest. RAP attempts to prepare students for productive careers, fulfilling personal lives, enlightened citizenship, and lifelong learning. Central to the learning community is a foundation course engaging students in a conversation about scholarship, fostering the building of information literacy skills, developing research abilities, and connecting students to the community through service learning. The main focus is on the development of research and communication skills, with special attention to becoming information literate, learning new technologies, and becoming familiar with a variety of perspectives. Moreover, students make connections across their curriculum and understand the link between theory and practice. The class is a hands-on collaborative environment with creative activities and discussion. Many service learning projects were developed over the fourteen years that this program has been in operation; the following four projects illustrate how service learning can enhance information literacy skills.

Museum Exhibits. COllaboratory was an initiative included as part of the foundation course for the program. The project brought together teams of college and K–12 students, museum staff, faculty, and others from around the country to create museum exhibits reflecting research on a yearly theme. This was not a traditional service learning setting. However, students reached out to K–12 students and helped them participate in a large research project that was then offered for viewing to the public.

*By doing this project it really brought out part of me
that I didn't know was in me.*

(first-year RAP student)

Students were connected via electronic mail and became members of Walden3, a virtual community that provided a text-based platform for virtual world building and synchronous communication. It provided an online venue for team members to access each other as well as museum staff, librarians, and faculty. One important component of COllaboratory was that it encouraged students to recognize that learning is an ongoing endeavor, that education is as much a process as a product, and that connecting to the rest of the world serves to broaden perspectives, enhances creativity, and nurtures intellectual inquiry.

> *I have learned so much about myself. I have learned so much about others. I have learned what it means to give. I have learned what it means to help. I have learned the meaning of the phrase, "do something." I have learned what it means to be patient. And I have learned not to take life for granted.*
>
> *(first-year RAP student)*

The museum exhibit projects were continued over a six-year period. "Celebrations" was the theme for one particular year of the program that illustrates the skills learned. The goal was for the students to learn a number of research strategies in their foundation course and then collaborate with K–12 students in their own community as well as with college students at the University of Southern Maine and K–12 students in Portland. Students worked in teams and did extensive research on the origins of various celebrations from around the world. They created "pathfinders," outlines of research possibilities for each of the celebrations. The pathfinders included research questions, reviews of the literature, methodologies, annotated bibliographies, and intended outcomes for the research. However, rather than complete a traditional research paper, the students worked with their K–12 and college partners to create exhibits. These exhibits were put on display at the Bishop Museum in Honolulu and then shipped to Portland, Maine, to their Museum of Art.

Students who participated in this rigorous project met many portions of all the information literacy standards. They conferred with instructors, worked in teams, identified key concepts, defined a realistic overall plan, and produced knowledge for public display. The project was aligned with Best Practices, as the mission was to integrate information literacy skills into a larger research project, the collaboration on the exhibit was between faculty and librarians, and the project reached out beyond the university into the community and beyond.

Kid's Kitchen. Kids' Kitchen was a community service project that was a partnership between the Rotary of Honolulu Sunrise, Harbor House, and RAP. Harbor House is a nonprofit charity providing food, clothing, and shelter to those in need. The Rotarians donated monies needed to pay for a site coordinator and offered assistance to the site with painting, building, and other activities, as needed.

> *I have interacted. I have maintained a positive attitude.*
> *I have had fun. I have learned. I have contributed. I*
> *have helped. I have fed and nourished the minds and*
> *stomachs of some children. I have changed.*
> *(first-year RAP student)*

Kids' Kitchen provided meals for young children who were left alone afternoons to fend for themselves. Up to thirty-five children, aged five to twelve, were offered meals each day. The school principal worked closely with the coordinator of the program to facilitate communication with the families. Each late afternoon, Monday through Friday, meals were prepared and served to the children. Additionally, volunteers (freshmen in RAP) became role models for the children. The college students encouraged youngsters to participate in various tabletop and recreational activities. Youngsters also were given opportunities to sit and "talk story," got assistance with their homework, and participated in lively discussions. Thus, volunteers not only provided supervision for the children during their meals but also provided nourishment for the youngsters' minds. Students who participated in Kids' Kitchen had life-changing experiences.

> *If I can change one kid's life, I can change the future.*
> *(first-year RAP student)*

This project was a more traditional service learning project in that students actually went to the site and served food as well as mentored young children. The articulation with the curriculum was through the program's foundation course. Students were conducting research on topics related to their work at Kid's Kitchen. They were made aware of the economic, legal, and social issues that arise when working with a community, especially with children from low-income families. In later semesters, the student research was actually applied to their work with the various agencies; however, in Kid's Kitchen, their learning came from the reflective journals they kept throughout the semester. They were able to make connections with what they were doing at the site and the reading they were doing in many of their general education classes (sociology, political science, psychology, and so on).

Literacy at Lincoln. Another project that engaged students in both working with children and conducting research was mentoring students at an elementary school. The focus was on helping improve reading skills. RAP students went to Lincoln Elementary School each week to read with and to the students. In their foundation course, they researched the concept of literacy and the multiple programs that have been developed over the years. Doing this research helped them design the methods by which they would work with the elementary students. In addition to the reading, students worked with Foodbank to assemble food boxes monthly. These were distributed to the families in the Lincoln Elementary neighborhood. This work helped connect the RAP students with both the children and their families, giving them insight into the socioeconomic status of the children.

Again, this project was a collaborative effort among librarians, faculty, and the community. The ability to reach out into the community exemplified the prevailing pedagogy of the program, which was to link the research skills they were learning to some aspect of the community in which they were living. Students needed to reflect on their own values, investigate differing viewpoints encountered in the literature, and maintain a journal or log of activities related to their information seeking.

Online Course. Most faculty and staff at institutions of higher learning grapple with limited time and personnel when trying to develop a new program. Sometimes organizational structure itself gets in the way of new ideas and projects. Thus, the concept of an online component and structure for service learning might be a good option. An e-learning environment makes resources accessible for students in terms of work and the exploration of information literacy skills. For teachers who do not think they have the time to include service learning, this electronic environment can offer choices for integration. For two years, the staffing of RAP was cut back and it was necessary to think of new ways to incorporate service learning. By giving most of the responsibility to the students and by putting the readings and reflective components of the course online, the projects were varied and successful. Students were asked to read a number of selections placed on a course Web site. They also were responsible for gathering additional information about service learning in general and issues in relation to their community agency specifically, which were shared on the Web site. Students wrote reflective e-journals weekly to document their two hours spent at an agency of their choice.

Thus, rather than conduct a project in which the entire class was involved, the students chose from among forty community agencies in setting up a working relationship throughout the semester. The mission of the program to involve students within the community was well served. In addition, the students were able to build their research skills by searching for relevant articles and materials to be shared with the class. A final project for each student was to actually conduct research for their particular agency and then do a poster presentation of their results and conclusions.

Thinktank. For the fall of 2005, students in RAP were invited to become part of a "thinktank" on education. The purpose was to explore answers to the question, Why college? In addition to readings, discussions, and think papers to be written, the students collaborated with Dole Middle School. This collaboration was part of a national project called The Century Program (affiliated with the Foundation for Excellent Schools) designed to help middle school students become what they call "college ready." The role of the RAP student was to tutor and mentor these middle school students, help them with goal setting, introduce them to the university by offering college tours, and invite them to participate in classes. The project was two-pronged. While exploring the purpose of a liberal education, the various arguments for and against traditional general education courses, the advent of new business ventures into higher education, and the goals they have set for themselves, the RAP students had to devise strategies that would persuade, prepare, and excite middle school students about the prospects of going to college. The activities involved included many discussions, both in class and on a listserv, weekly "think" papers responding to readings, weekly student presentations on topics of their choice, and the development of the various projects with the Dole students. They had to storyboard ideas, plan events, research laws (for instance, the No Child Left Behind Act), participate in online discussion formats, and communicate clearly to each other and to middle school students. All these activities led to increased information literacy competencies.

Concluding Remarks

> *To be information literate is to be able to take all that*
> *you pick up, with your senses or hands, and to have the*
> *power to read it like a book. To be information literate*
> *is to be able to read life like a book.*
>   Brent Buchanon (first-year student)

In *Leadership and the New Science,* Margaret Wheatley used chaos theory
as a construct to study organizations and leadership. She suggested that we
need to move away from the machine model of thinking, the one in which
we believe that studying the parts will automatically lead to comprehension
of the whole. She further suggested that the new science is a holistic way
of thinking, replacing the Newtonian model and giving primary value to
relationships that exist.[18] To answer the questions posed by Edmundson,
students need to make connections between and among all the different
content areas. The essence of becoming educated is in the ability to make
meaning of these relationships.

> *How we choose to believe and speak and treat others,*
> *how we choose a civic role for ourselves, is the deepest*
> *purpose of a liberal education and of the act of*
> *teaching.*
>   A. Bartlett Giamatti

Richard J. Light interviewed students for over ten years and reported in
Making the Most of College that most students are interested in having faculty
"make connections between serious curriculum on the one hand, and the
students' personal lives, values, and experiences, on the other."[19] Somehow
students have an intrinsic understanding that a college education needs to
be connected to real life. John Dewey recognized that understanding early
on and suggested that active student involvement in learning is an essential
element in effective education. In his book, *Experience and Education,* he
stated that "there is one permanent frame of reference; namely, the organic
connection between education and personal experience."[20]

Thus, if becoming information literate is key to becoming an educated
person, it follows that the integration of service learning possibilities, be

they integrated into a semester course or just short-term projects, infuses the students' experiences with opportunities to make those connections between what they are learning and their personal experience. Service learning, by its very nature, contributes to students' ability to understand when new knowledge is needed, where they might find it, how they might determine if what they find is actually credible and/or helpful, and, finally, how they might communicate what they learned in a manner that actually gets something done.

There are many literacies that we hope are developed in students over their time in a formal educational environment. First of all, traditional literacy (reading and writing) itself is key, and then students must grasp mathematical, visual, media, computer, and information literacies. Integrating service learning into regular courses, into first-year experience courses, or perhaps into smaller workshops helps students further develop all these literacies.

Notes

1. Mark Edmunson, Why Read (New York: Bloomsbury Publishing, 2004), 5.

2. Arthur Levine and Jeanette S. Cureton, When Hope and Fear Collide (San Francisco: Jossey-Bass, 1998).

3. Neil Postman, The End of Education (New York: Vintage Books, 1995).

4. Wingspread Group on Higher Education, An American Imperative: Higher Expectations for Higher Education (Wisconsin: The Johnson Foundation, 1993), 11.

5. George D. Kuh, "Conceptual Framework and Overview of Psychometric Properties," The National Survey of Student Engagement.

6. Ernest L. Boyer, Reinventing Undergraduate Education (The Boyer Commission, 1998), 16.

7. A.W. Chickering and Z.F. Gamson, "Seven Principles for Good Practice in Undergraduate Education," AHHE Bulletin 39, no. 7 (1987): 39.

8. Howard Radest, Community Service: Encounter with Strangers (Connecticut: Praeger, 1993), 139.

9. Robert N. Bellah, Habits of the Heart (New York: Harper & Row, 1985), 293.

10. Mary Catherine Bateson, Peripheral Visions (New York: Harper Collins, 1994), 12.

11. Jaques Barzun, Begin Here: The Forgotten Conditions of Teaching and Learning (Chicago: University of Chicago Press, 1991).

12. Ernest L. Boyer, College: The Undergrdauate Experience in America (New York: Harper & Row, 1987), 83.

13. Ibid., 214.

14. Alan S. Waterman, Service-Learning: Applications from the Research (New Jersey: Lawrence Erlbaum Associates, 1997), 70.

15. Ilene F. Rockman and Associates, Integrating Information Literacy Into the Higher Education Curriculum (San Francisco: Jossey-Bass, 2004), 1.

16. Patricia Senn Breivik, "Information Literacy and the Engaged Campus," AAHE Bulletin (Nov. 2000): 4.

17. Rockman, Integrating Information Literacy Into the Higher Education Curriculum, 61.

18. Margaret Wheatley, Leadership and the New Science (San Francisco: Berrett-Koehler, 1992), 8.

19. Richard J. Light, Making the Most of College: Students Speak Their Minds (Cambridge: Harvard University Press, 2001), 110.

20. John Dewey, Experience and Education (New York: Simon & Schuster, 1997), 25.

Ways of Thinking: Doing Research and Being Information Literate

Randy Burke Hensley

Student engagement is about finding a relationship between what college does and what students value. At its essence, college exposes students to ways of thinking about the world, past, present, and future. These ways of thinking are examined through processes of discovering how information becomes knowledge and how data are transformed into meaning. The mechanism for these processes is research. Information literacy can be understood as the articulation of learning outcomes for teaching how to do research. These outcomes can become personal characteristics, ways that students define who they are and how they think.

The traditional curriculum of the American institution of higher education, be it survey course or laboratory, theory or practice, methodology or service learning, addresses the standard components of the research process. Often, however, the student experience of the curriculum does not lend itself to an understanding of, and ability to engage with, these components—or even a basic understanding of what knowledge is and how scholars and researchers create it. They usually "get" what knowledge is because they are asked to habitually regurgitate it but seem mystified, at least as undergraduates, by the notion that knowledge is created by means of a dynamic questioning, discovery, and evaluative conversation: a discourse. Students do not understand research as the central construction of knowledge. They certainly do not understand research as a broadly applicable cognitive process for problem solving in their daily lives. Most important, they do not perceive research as the embodiment of values and personal characteristics they should want as their own.

Teaching research, properly formulated and understood, to first-year undergraduate students can foster in them the desire to learn because research is an invitation to become someone most students want to be: thoughtful, aware, curious, creative, effective, and flexible.

Fixing the Learning Arena: College
In making the case for the centrality of teaching research as the foundational paradigm for college teaching and learning, student engagement, and information literacy, it is necessary to examine what is going on, or not, at college.

Mel Scarlett's *The Great Rip-Off in American Education: Undergrads Underserved* begins where so many critiques of American higher education do: the Boyer Commission's *Reinventing Undergraduate Education: A Blueprint for America's Research Universities.* "The first priority of the University is research, and in the campus reward systems, decisions about tenure, promotion, and salary are based primarily, if not entirely, on the quality and quantity of a faculty member's research. Consequently, faculty are likely to give major emphasis and most of their time to their research—to the detriment of their teaching of undergraduates. The predominant teaching method used is still the lecture, in which the student is a passive listener. This in spite of what research shows: students learn much better when they are active participants in the learning process."[1] Research is at the center of college, but not in the right way for the right people.

Again, referring to the Boyer Commission Report, Scarlett states, "Inquiry-based learning is recommended instead of the usual lecture method. According to the Boyer Commission report, 'the basic idea of learning as inquiry is the same as research; even though advanced research occurs at advanced levels, undergraduates beginning in the freshman year can learn through research…in a setting in which inquiry is prized, every course in an undergraduate curriculum should provide an opportunity for a student to succeed through discovery-based methods.'"[2] Scarlett and the

Boyer Commission view research as a dynamic context for achieving an understanding of knowledge, what is known as well as how that knowledge is achieved. Notice how close to the standard definitions of information literacy the following excerpt from the Boyer Report is, Scarlett asserts that "all the skills of research developed in earlier work should be marshaled in a project that demands the framing of a significant question or set of questions, the research or creative exploration to find answers, and the communication skills to convey the results to audiences both expert and uninitiated in the subject matter."[3]

Scarlett continues his critique by examining a number of governance issues of higher education. However, he continues the view of research and teaching as dichotomous: "The production of significant research should continue, but the dominance of research over teaching must be altered."[4] Furthermore, "the requirement for all faculty to be productive publishing researchers must be eliminated. Those who can and wish to produce significant research should be encouraged to do so."[5]

But what if research is the core content of any course? Then faculty's research is the teaching. We teach from and to our research. Students can participate in the gathering of data, the critiquing of findings, the review of the literature, the verification of any number of aspects of any research process. Research already completed can be used to teach the creation of knowledge process, with faculty being unusually informed of the strengths and weaknesses of their own work as well as the discourse for that work. Finally, research must be infused with the type of credibility that makes it relevant to the practical, everyday world students inhabit. Faculty doing research can provide an effective bridge between theoretical and practical by teaching from research they have actually done, then guiding students through possible applications to life situations.

Can librarians teach from a research paradigm? Yes. Many librarians have done—and continue to do—research with social science and humanities methodologies predominant in the literature. However, librarians may be uniquely qualified to teach from a research perspective because of their strengths as interdisciplinary inquirers.

Their ability to cross traditional disciplinary boundaries in the formation of collections, access devices, and in the provision of "inquiry" (reference) assistance to information seekers is well acknowledged. Furthermore, librarians, many of whom are considered faculty on their campuses, understand the questioning and literature review areas within the research process as core to the performance of traditional librarian responsibilities.

In his 2005 book, *Universities As If Students Mattered,* John Scanzoni examines the need for a change in the way we teach. Like Scarlett, he supports the shift from a content-driven curriculum to a research- and inquiry-driven one and sees this shift as historically grounded: "the influential twentieth-century pragmatic philosopher John Dewey (followed later by a number of other 'progressive' thinkers) argued that learning happens best in the context of 'reflective thinking.' And one learns how to think (analyze, evaluate, synthesize) by doing—specifically, trying to solve a problem, that is, seeking to answer a question."[6] He imagines the undergraduate curriculum as one "devoted to the design of research aimed to change the conditions of social life in certain limited ways. And when appropriate, the student would get actual hands-on experience by participating in the research and in making sense of the actual findings. But, at other times, the execution and interpretation might be done via simulation or a hypothetical mock-up of what might transpire if the project were actually carried out."[7]

Scanzoni spends a great deal of time making the case for social science as the primary modality for transforming the university because of its disciplinary focus on the nature of the social world. Social science research develops knowledge for improving the human condition so students will become invested in research that they see as improving their own circumstances.

He makes two more points that are relevant to this discussion. "The capability of making knowledge is seen as the essence of the post-industrial information age. And persons who are skilled at doing that can be expected to do well in the twenty-first century—both in the marketplace and in civic society."[8] Furthermore, "problem solving and the cultivation of human capital skills are team-based. Peers learn from each other. And, although the coach is presumably more experienced in and capable than the players and the interns (grad students and postdocs) at such problem solving, the coaches fully expect to learn from and to grow alongside the players and interns."[9]

In summation, fixing college involves centralizing the research process in the curriculum, modifying pedagogy to be more inquiry based, problem based, discovery based in a learning community setting so that questioning, analytical, and evaluative abilities provide context for appropriate content knowledge. The attributes of information literacy are a natural fit as a succinct articulation of learning outcomes for this process. But will this transformation engage students? Is it what they want from college?

Student Engagement…Like It Mattered

For Bridget D. Arend, "engagement, defined simply as the time and effort spent on activities, has become an established means of understanding the experience and quality of student learning in higher education. It is measured by using specific behaviors such as discussing class material or participating in co-curricular activities."[10] However, for those of us who have attempted class discussions, getting students to discuss content or express personal perspectives can be both trying and disappointing in getting students to develop their own ideas and examine different points of view, or even participate at all. The key, as Arthur Sandeen points out in his book, *Enhancing Student Engagement on Campus,* is to facilitate a classroom where "some of the best learning occurs as a result of trial and error, and [where] there is rarely a good substitute for self-discovery."[11] His experience as a student affairs administrator also has shown a relationship between various forms of campus involvement by students and a more active form of ownership of the experience of the curriculum that transforms the student. He points out that integration of college experiences can create students who make more personal meaning out of their college decisions. He observes, "moreover, many students select college majors and professional careers to impress friends and family, or, simply to gain their acceptance or admiration."[12] Students who are enabled to interact more with their campuses and curricula report greater satisfaction with the college experience. Sandeen concludes, "students must be free, as well to read, to study, and to pursue academic, social, and political issues if they are to learn effectively. Students learn to accept responsibility by having it, and they learn about the truth in an atmosphere of free inquiry, debate, and discussion."[13]

The result of this freedom and responsibility to inquire accomplishes a quite traditional outcome of a college education, according to George D. Kuh and Paul D. Umbach. "The college experience was intended to shape student attitudes and values as much as stretch their intellect and expand their knowledge of the world."[14] Offering a curriculum that inquires as to how we know what we know, providing processes for questioning that knowledge and creating new knowledge, must call into play students' understanding of what they already know and from whence that knowledge comes. Students begin to understand themselves both as an "I" and a "thou." This personality transformation happens through student interaction with academic and out-of-class activities that can be designed to be educationally significant. In fact, the National Survey of Student Engagement, *The College Student Report,* asks students about the amount of time and effort devoted to various in-class and out-of-class experiences, participation in enriching educational activities, gains in personal and educational development, and perceptions of the college environment.

The Kuh and Umbach study sought to demonstrate a relationship among these activities and perceived academic challenge, active and collaborative learning pedagogy, and student–faculty interaction.[15] Kuh and Umbrach offer this assessment: "As Sweet Briar College president Elisabeth Muhlenfeld said, the NSSE items represent 'an effort to get at the habits of mind.'"[16] Courses that integrate knowledge with their lives produce students that are engaged in learning.

Alongside new approaches to teaching and learning, new tools for learning can impact students. Technology, which has affected the storage and accessing of information and libraries, has demonstrated an ability to engage students. Bridget D. Arend's study "revealed that patters of engagement are changing due to the use of personal computing, yet many institutional services are barely keeping up with high student expectations for technology, let along capitalizing on the learning opportunities inherent in the technology."[17] Technology needs to be used not just to communicate and retrieve, but also to explore and create. It should be considered a thorough and integrated attribute of college courses. "Here the goal is not simply to use technology to automate what we already do but to take advantage of innovations to change our work and make that work better."[18]

Along with technology, Richard J. Light discusses the importance of writing to student engagement. His study concluded, "the results are stunning. The relationship between the amount of writing for a course and students' level of engagement—whether engagement is measured by time spent on the course, or the intellectual challenge it presents, or students' level of interest in it—is stronger than the relationship between students' engagement and any other course characteristic."[19] Light illuminates a specific kind of writing, what I call inquiry writing, as most effective. Students themselves "urge more writing instruction in a substantive context."[20] He clarifies by stating, "the frustration occurs when a teacher seems to forget whose paper it is, and begins to change the voice of an essay from the student's voice to the teacher's voice."[21] Students who are asked to engage a learning process that requires writing as demonstration and artifact of their own inquiry are more likely to report both learning and engagement.

In order to actually design or redesign courses that better relate to students and their learning needs, Stephen Bowen has offered an articulation of student engagement that can serve as hallmarks for courses. "The most fundamental is *student engagement with the learning process*: just getting students actively involved. The second is *student engagement with the object of study*. Here the emphasis is on stimulation of students' learning by direct experience of something new.

> Another is *student engagement with contexts* of the subject of study. This gives emphasis to the importance of context as it may affect and be affected by the students' primary subject. Finally, there is *student engagement with the human condition*, especially in its social, cultural, and civic dimensions. According to this way of thinking, the human condition is the ultimate subject of study to which individual subjects and disciplines should be understood as subordinate.[22]

A research- or inquiry-based curriculum can enhance student engagement because it can incorporate a variety of activities to integrate experience, knowledge, and personal values so that ongoing transformation of an ever-changing context for living in the world becomes possible. Technology and writing are primary pedagogical mechanisms for teaching such a curriculum. Information literacy is the articulation of abilities necessary to succeed in such a curriculum.

How The University of Hawaii Inquiry Course Works

A specific course from the first-year curriculum of the University of Hawaii at Manoa can serves as a specific model for teaching research to engage students. For four years, LIS100: Libraries, Scholarship, & Technology has been offered to first-year undergraduate students. In 2001, it received the Association of College & Research Libraries, Instruction Section, Innovation in Instruction Award (http://libweb.hawaii.edu/uhmlib/learnlib/learnlib.html# lis100). LIS 100 is a semester-long, three-credit course designated to fulfill general education requirements for writing. It is limited to twenty-five students a semester per section and has been regularly taught in a learning community composed of a service learning course and an American studies survey course.

The student learning outcomes for the course in 2005 were:

- Understand and demonstrate the differences of and relationship between information and knowledge
- Understand the elements of personal narrative
- Understand the elements of scholarly narrative
- Develop information literacy by being able to:
  — Create successful information searching strategies
  — Find information sources for specific purposes and audiences
  — Critically evaluate information sources
  — Incorporate information for specific purposes
  — Acknowledge information sources and provide citations
- Develop a work of scholarship by applying the elements of scholarly narrative to a research project

The course design is based on the conceptual framework of "story." The course assumes that life comprises stories, all kinds. Students are in the process of creating the story of their lives. Scholarship in the form of research is simply a story told with a particular set of conventions. It is intended that if students can appreciate research as another kind of story among many different kinds of stories with which they are already familiar, their ability to comprehend and create such stories is enhanced.

The course uses Margit Misangyi Watts's *College: We Make the Road by Walking* as its primary text. How does LIS100 address the attributes previously considered as important for inquiry, student engagement, and information literacy? It does so through the incorporation of what are termed *conceptual components* integrated through learning activities leading to a series of benchmark projects.

Asking Questions

Students are given a number of newspaper articles to analyze according to what questions are being answered and what questions need to be answered. In addition, they are asked to find information sources that answer those questions and to determine what additional questions arise from those answers. They also are taken through an understanding of what hypotheses are by generating hypotheses from questions. They are taught that hypotheses are possible solutions to a problem. In order to create a solution questions are possible solutions to a problem. In order to create a solution questions must be asked about the problem.

Research Elements

Hypothesis, methodology, literature review, data (results), interpretation, significance, and references become habitual hallmarks of thinking, writing, discussion, and understanding. Students learn to comprehend them through parallels with the following elements of storytelling: main character, trouble coming (plot complications), crisis, insight, affirmation.[23] Students learn to appreciate that literature reviews are what they used to call research, but, in fact, they constitute the context for the new knowledge they are creating through the research process. Furthermore, the literature review is evaluated by a process of determining the credibility (reputation) and validity (evidence for author perspective) of each source in order to be included as relevant to the student's research.

Values, Perspectives, and Significant Information

Students arrive at college with perspectives seldom more nuanced than dichotomous notions of belief. They are asked to explore the relationship among personal values and how they form particular perspectives on issues that lead to perceptions and filtering of what information is experienced, retrieved, or known. The most recent course used a reading of Gregory Maguire's *Wicked* and the viewing of the 1939 film *The Wizard of Oz* as texts to create a mock scholarly narrative articulating a personal perspective about Elphaba, the "Wicked Witch of the West." Students also are asked to find additional sources that can be used to illuminate their scholarship.

Clarity, Coherence, Creativity, and Correct

Students are required to do a minimum of sixteen pages of evaluated writing in the course. All writing is assessed against the "4C's" standard. Is word choice accurate and sufficiently descriptive for the meaning intended? Are sentences and paragraphs constructed and related to one another so that meaning is achieved? Have novel ideas and insights been included? Does the writing meet standards for English grammar? These standards encourage students to incorporate creative thinking as an essential component of how they write.

Active Learning

The pedagogy emphasizes student activity. Presentation of information rarely exceeds twenty-minutes at any one time. A model of experience, practice, and application is regularly followed. This model requires some activity that asks the student to recall their own experiences of the topic. New information requires an opportunity for students to practice their comprehension of that information. An application activity is given to guide the retention of information, transforming it to learning where students can use the information for a new purpose in the future. Peer activities and peer evaluations are used regularly, especially as a component of the writing revisions. Early in the course, students are placed in research teams that last for most of the semester so that the research is accomplished through the use of collaborative learning techniques while offering possibilities for sustained involvement with research questions significant to students.

Links to Campus and Community

The service learning course produces the problems for research. Students are asked to identify a problem from their service learning environment that needs a solution. Curiosity, personal interest, and the ability for students to create new knowledge through a research process of approximately twelve weeks are the selection criteria. Students have completed research projects for improving public radio marketing, enhancing the educational roles of nature centers, and improving elementary school tutoring programs.

Research Teams

Research teams develop each segment of the research projects with benchmarks established for drafts, peer and instructor review, and completion. Students improve their oral presentation abilities by meeting requirements for class demonstrations of database searching, methodologies, and initial findings. These latter "work in progress" presentations are based on the scholarly construct of conference papers. They support an understanding of the dynamic nature of knowledge creation by fostering an environment where researchers invite questions and alternative perspectives on their work. The research teams conclude their work with the writing of a research journal–quality paper that replicates the form and function of a journal article.

Ethics
Students learn to respect the process of attribution and ethical use of information by linking the perspective of ownership on knowledge and knowing with evaluating the worth of information, knowledge, and ideas. Avoiding plagiarism becomes a desired outcome of research because students develop a desire to own the ideas and knowledge they create. When determining credibility and validity, they want to attribute their sources as part of deciding that a source will be used to support their own research or rejected for weaknesses. They become critics and achieve the ability to operate in the world of information flow and sources in an enabled and analytical manner. They can decide who is good and who is not.

Application
To ensure that students understand that knowledge creation and research are not static artifacts of academia but, rather, dynamic ways to think about the world and solve problems, they are asked to individually create something from their team research findings. Students have created letters to administrators about campus problems, developed brochures and video training materials, and created songs and Web sites.

Throughout the course, computer technology and writing are used to enhance the learning environment, to foster creativity, and to ground the theoretical nature of research in practical uses of knowledge, ensuring that the distinction between data and meaning is grasped.

These conceptual components provide a mechanism for constant invigoration of student engagement by allowing for refocusing of activity toward student interests as they emerge during the learning process. In essence, the course "inquires about inquiry" by encouraging students to stay close to the forging of a relationship between personal immediate interests and long-term usefulness of the research approach to solving problems. Students practice becoming critical thinkers of the content of their research as well as the process of research itself. The emphasis in the course on the use of information technology as part of the learning process and writing as the chief artifact of what they discover further serves to address the attributes of student engagement previously discussed by Light and others.

Conclusion
Students are engaged when they can participate in learning that they can

understand as being important to who they want to be in the world. Content in the service of the research process accomplishes the need for students to be lifelong participants in solving problems. Life is a series of problems needing solutions. Providing students with ways of thinking so that they can learn to solve problems will best enable them to be present in the college learning experience and successful in their lives after college. When its hallmarks become attributes of thinking rather than a skills set, information literacy becomes the core of inquiry and research.

Notes

1. Mel Scarlett, The Great Rip-Off in American Education: Undergrads Underserved (Amherst, NY: Prometheus Books, 2004).

2. Ibid., 29.

3. Ibid., 31.

4. Ibid., 102.

5. Ibid., 103.

6. John Scanzoni, Universities As If Students Mattered (Lanham, MD: Rowman Littlefield Publisher, Inc., 2005), 10.

7. Ibid., 11.

8. Ibid., 169.

9. Ibid.

10. Bridget D. Arend, "New Patterns of Student Engagement," About Campus (July–Aug. 2004): 30–32.

11. Arthur Sandeen, Enhancing Student Engagement on Campus (Lanham, MD: University Press of American, 2003), 28.

12. Ibid., 30.

13. Ibid., 68.

14. Kuh, George D., and Paul D. Umbach, "College and Character: Insights from the National Survey of Student Engagement," New Directions for Institutional Research 122 (summer 2004): 37–54.

15. Ibid., 40.

16. Ibid., 39.

17. Arend, "New Patterns of Student Engagement," 31.

18. Ibid., 32.

19. Richard J. Light, "Writing and Students' Engagement," AAC&U Peer Review (fall 2003): 28–31.

20. Ibid., 31.

21. Ibid.

22. Bowen, Stephen, "Engaged Learning: Are We All on the Same Page?" AAC&U Peer Review (winter 2005): 4–7.

23. Donald Davis, Telling Your Own Stories (Little Rock, AK: August House Publishers, 1993).

Bibliography

Arend, Bridget D., "New Patterns of Student Engagement: Lessons from a Laptop University," *About Campus* (July–Aug. 2004): 30–32.

Bowen, Stephen, "Engaged Learning: Are We All on the Same Page?" *Association of American Colleges and Universities, PeerReview* (winter 2005): 4–7.

Davis, Donald, *Telling Your Own Stories* (Little Rock, AK: August House Publishers, 1993).

Handelsman, Mitchell M., William L.Briggs, Nora Sullivan, and Annette Towler, "A Measure of College Student Course Engagement," *Journal of Educational Research* 98 (Jan./Feb. 2005): 184–91.

Kuh, George D., and Paul D. Umbach, "College and Character: Insights from the National Survey of Student Engagement," *New Directors for Institutional Research* 122 (summer 2004): 37–54.

Light, Richard J., "Writing and Students' Engagement," *Association of American Colleges and Universities Peer Review* (fall 2003): 28–31.

Maguire, Gregory, *Wicked: The Life and Times of the Wicked Witch of the West* (New York: ReganBooks, HarperCollins Publishers, 1995).

Sandeen, Arthur, *Enhancing Student Engagement on Campus* (Lanham, MD: University Press of America, 2003).

Scanzoni, John, *Universities as if Students Mattered* (Lanham, MD: Rowman & Littlefield Publishers, 2005).

Scarlett, Mel, *The Great Rip-Off in American Education: Undergrads Underserved* (Amherst, NY: Prometheus Books, 2004), 24.

Watts, Margit Misangyi, *College: We Make the Road by Walking* (Upper Saddle River, NJ: Prentice-Hall, 2003).

Wizard of Oz (New York: MGM/UA Home Video, 1983, c1939).

The Winds of Change: Generation Y, Student Learning, and Assessment in Higher Education

Patricia Davitt Maughan

E very other year, the University of California, Los Angeles's School of Education and Information Studies hosts fifteen senior fellows and provides them with the opportunity to reflect on their work and to study individual and collective interests relating to librarianship. In 2003, the fellows chose to replicate and update the work of Deborah Grimes, who studied the centrality of academic libraries to their home institutions. They interviewed the presidents and provosts of six universities with student bodies that ranged in size from fifteen to twenty-eight thousand and library collections that ranged in size from 1.3 to five million volumes. They asked these leaders, "When is the library a top priority?"

Presidents responded that it is when library matters emerge as part of campus strategic planning; provosts said it is when they hear complaints or problems with the library. The presidents and provosts interviewed commonly viewed the library as a depository, a physical space, a psychological center for the university, a social and working place for students, and a campus site for reliable information. A few mentioned the role of library as publisher. Within their comments, there seems to be a glaring omission of the library's campus educational partner that can meaningfully contribute to the goal and assessment of student learning. These academic leaders viewed libraries as an "odd man out," noting that libraries do not ask for budgets in the same way that other departments and academic units do (e.g., by linking their budget requests to student enrollments). This suggests that the educational role of the library is largely unrecognized and overlooked. Presidents and provosts also noted the importance of assessment and commented on the lack of high-quality data linking library collections and services to the campus's research and educational accomplishments. The fellows concluded that a major shift in library attributes and centrality indicators needs to occur before libraries will be viewed as "key players" at their home institutions. In developing strategies, products, and collaborations with faculty and other campus learning experts, and documenting their collective impact on student learning, libraries need to re-envision their role and become a more integral part of the teaching and learning enterprise.

Libraries are cultural, social, political, and intellectual institutions that, if they are to be effective and valued, must understand and respond to the changes and forces present in the larger communities in which they exist. Academic libraries are not only situated on college and university campuses, but also within the realm of higher education as a whole. They must continually scan these environments for changes and plan to respond accordingly, or in some cases to lead change, if they are to ensure their continued viability. Changes in today's higher education front are evident in three critical areas: in the learning and behavior characteristics of today's college students, in higher education's shift in emphasis to student-centered and active learning approaches to education, and in the growing accountability movement within public and higher education institutions. This chapter explores these changes and discusses selected implications they have for libraries, while suggesting approaches and strategies that libraries can employ to ensure that they change in concert with their larger academic environments and thus demonstrably add value to both student learning and institutional effectiveness.

A Portrait of Generation Y

> I see the library as, like, this place with lots of books, that were written very long ago in the past.[1]

Instructors generally acknowledge that understanding their students is an important part of instructional design, one that is critical to student learning and engagement. Special efforts are required from today's instructors to achieve this understanding, however, because most instructors populate a different generation than do many of their students. This difference is concisely stated by Karen Hein, past president of the William T. Grant Foundation, who writes, "If there is a digital divide, it is between the generations."[2]

Many or most of today's students, alternately referred to as Generation Y, Net Gens, or Millennials (born between 1979 and 1994), have grown up in a world increasingly populated by interactive video games, computers, the Web, instant messaging (IM), and cellular phones. Professor Jeff Cole, who is currently engaged in a study of the impact of the Internet on society, notes that for the first time since television was introduced some fifty years ago, television viewing among young people has decreased. Internet use has replaced it, a finding that he attributes to the lure of the Internet's *interactivity*. It is currently estimated that Generation Y spends an average of eleven hours per week online.[3]

Increasingly, Millennials are adapting to what older generations call "newer technologies" to increase their levels of interconnectivity, to communicate, and to socialize. In contrast to preceding generations, Generation Y takes these tools in stride. More than 17 million teenagers were reported to be online in 2001 and three-quarters of them use IM regularly. A typical Millennial might have from 100 to 200 IM buddies. For this new generation, online communication is, in many cases, as meaningful as face-to-face conversation.

They describe themselves as being able to identify and use a range of technologies better than most of their teachers. A 21-year-old student from the California Polytechnic University, recently interviewed by the *New York Times*, noted,

> My favorite gadget is my cell phone ... It has ... a wireless connection that lets me link to ... my Pocket PC ... I can connect directly from my Pocket PC to my phone to the Internet ... my Pocket PC is my Palm Pilot and my iPod in one ... I tend to try to digitize all my class work so I take my lecture notes and scan them into my computer ... all that is hooked into my wireless network ... which lets me roam the house ... and watch TV while surfing the Internet or print[4]

A senior from the University of Connecticut commented,

> I don't go anywhere without my cell phone and digital camera …
> Last spring, I 'got one of the printers that has a copier-scanner …
> I don't ever go to the library now. I copy everything in my room
> … I send text messages while I'm in class … Last month, I sent
> over 2,000 text messages.[5]

Other Net Gen characteristics have been described by a number of researchers. (See table 1.) Hein delineates seven key traits of Millennials: "they feel special, sheltered, confident, team-oriented, achieving, pressured, and conventional."[6] With increasing focus on achievement, occasioned in part by the accountability movement in higher education, the majority of today's students say they have developed five- or ten-year plans for their future.[7] Their orientation toward achievement may manifest itself in their desire for rules, structure, priorities, and procedures in lieu of ambiguity. "Following the

Table 1. Selective Statistics on Today's Students **Demographics | Favored Technologies | Behaviors**	
% of students	**who...**
94%	Use the Internet for school research *Source: Oblinger 2003, 39.*
85%	Report owning their own computer *Source: Jones 2002, 2.*
75%	Use e-mail for explanations of assignments *Source: Jones 2002, 9.*
74%	Use IM (instant messaging) *Source: Lenhart 2001, 3.*
73%	Use the Internet *more* than the library for research needs *Source: Jones 2002, 3.*
73%	Are nontraditional students (delayed enrollment, enrolled part-time, work full-time, have dependents, single parents, etc.) *Source: Oblinger 2003, 38.*
39%	Are over the age of 25 *Source: Oblinger 2003, 38.*
25%	Own *more* than one computer *Source: Oblinger 2003, 39.*
9%	Use the library *more* than the Internet for information seeking *Source: Jones 2002, 3.*

rules, working really hard, not messing up—that's the common Millennial credo."[8] Pushed to study hard, as they perceive themselves to be, they may avoid taking personal risks in their learning, unless encouraged to do so and provided with structure and guidance. Carie Windham, a young woman who provides "The Student's Perspective" in Oblinger and Oblinger's *Educating the Net Generation,* puts it this way:

> Net Geners, for the most part, are not just driven by the notion of achievement – they are consumed by it.[9]

A second trait she notes is this:

> With information and accessibility lying effortless at my fingertips, I have grown accustomed to juggling multiple tasks at once, at lightning speed.[10]

In 2003, the University of California, Los Angeles Cooperative Institutional Research Program's study of first-year students identified many of these same traits in the Net Gens. To these, they added that Millennials expect instability, are "change ready," and are *focused on transferable skills.*

Many Generation Ys are *accustomed to learning online.* The U.S. Department of Education reports roughly one-third of all public high schools now offer some form of online distance education.[11] Windham comments,

> Most [students] log on to online courses because they despise ... [the] ... traditional format of lecture and regurgitate. Instead they feel they can learn better in an environment where they can teach themselves ... the online professor must find ways to offer students a method of exploration and research within the curriculum.[12]

In addition to being interconnected, Generation Y *makes extensive use of multimedia.* Researchers have noted that Net Gens are accomplished at "reading" visual images, *learn better through discovery* than by "being told," are skilled in shifting their attention quickly from task to task, respond rapidly to stimuli, and will decide not to pay attention to what does not interest them.

Windham characterizes her generation as follows:

> We want to learn about subjects through exploration. It is not enough for us to accept a professor's word. Instead, we want to be challenged to reach our own conclusions and find our own results.[13]

Jason Frand underscores this point when noting that today's students expect their education to *highlight the learning process* rather than a canon of knowledge. He further notes that Net Gens want to join active campus learning communities.[14]

Today's "teaching generation" and its "learning generation" differ from one another with respect to their preferred modes of learning. Where an older generation of faculty, librarians, and other academics generally prefer reading texts, researchers have noted that NetGens, raised on a steady diet of multimedia, retain significantly more of what they see than of what they read. Mark Prensky describes Generation Y as:

> children raised with the computer [who] think differently from the rest of us. They develop hypertext minds. They leap around.[15]

Because of their steady diet of visual media, Net Gens' textual literacy may be less well developed than that of preceding generations. The authors of "Preparing the Academy of Today for the Learner of Tomorrow," published in Oblinger and Oblingers' *Educating the Net Generation*, note a range of challenges to today's educators, including what they describe as Net Gens' shallow reading habits, relative *lack of critical thinking and evaluative skills*, and lack of understanding surrounding *issues of intellectual property*. Researchers have reported on the Millennials' frequent refusal to read lengthy instructions or lengthy course reading assignments.

Rather than reading widely for background information or consulting manuals as previous generations were inclined to do, they *prefer to experiment* and discover what works and what does not. Some believe Millennials' learning more closely resembles Nintendo than it does anything involving linearity or logic. The key to winning games such as Nintendo involves constant and persistent trial and error. Some educators, in fact, worry whether today's students are prepared to engage in more in-depth analysis when trial-and-error methods fail.

Researchers note that the traditionally linear approach to learning is much less common among Net Gens than is "bricolage," or the ability to piece together *information from multiple sources.* Generation Y is more oriented to inductive discovery, which involves formulating hypotheses, making observations, and teasing out of rules.

Generation Y and Information Use

In an informal fall 2005 survey, a small group of undergraduates at the University of California, Berkeley, were asked what "being college educated" signified to them. Their responses included the following:

- "Being educated is more than what one gets out of a text book or even out of a lecture."
- "To be educated means to … have the experience of the world. Not just classroom knowledge …"
- "[It] means having received a higher level of understanding in a given area of study. This includes having had practice [in] the skill of using resources provided, to better that understanding."
- "being able to think critically. If a 'college educated' person is presented with a problem/question, he/she can analyze the information presented … and come up with a rational answer."
- "Being educated means that you've been exposed to new ideas, different than those that you are comfortable with. Education is not just learned in the academic setting of the classroom …"

The role for the library as an out-of-classroom learning environment and learning experience is clear here. However, the ways in which libraries are currently organized to offer their services and the lack of student skills in conducting library research pose significant challenges, particularly when considered in light of student expectations.

In a 2004 University of California, Berkeley Library–produced video, Berkeley undergraduates had this to say about library research:

- "I don't think I knew how to really go about it, besides doing something on the Internet, 'cause I think the Internet is just more … maybe it's a generational thing … the Internet is really something easy for me to move around in and find things."

- "using the library actually is sometimes more difficult, being a student with a million classes because you, you know, have a tendency to just easily go to the Internet and type something in and find some information that you can probably expand on in the library, but, with time and everything, I've just found that it's actually more difficult despite the really good resources."[16]

These responses suggest significant implications for the provision of library services to Gen Y as well as for instructing them in library research and information literacy or fluency.

Although two-thirds of Net Gens report they know how to find valid information on the Web, they still recognize that the Web fails to meet all their information needs.[17] The national College Student Experiences Questionnaire (CSEQ) found that students spend as much time on the Internet as they do studying, yet only 50 percent of them expressed confidence in their abilities to find good information or to navigate a modern library. The same was true for their abilities to evaluate the accuracy and quality of the information they find. A study at Colorado State University found that 58 percent of freshmen relied on *an Internet search engine as their first strategy* for finding information; only 23 percent started with a library database or index.[18] A survey at Southwestern University revealed that students indeed recognized that they floundered when searching for materials to meet their research needs and wasted a great deal of time in their efforts to do so.[19] Other researchers have found that Millennials tend to gloss over issues surrounding the owners or publishers of sources, and frequently *focus primarily on activities that lead to a classroom grade.*[20]

What more is known of this new cohort of learners? They often express the belief that *anything accessible online should be free.* In their minds, the lines between creators of information and consumers of information are blurred. They often assume that if information is digital, it can be used freely without need for attribution. In the absence of receiving instruction to the contrary, many Millennials see *nothing wrong with plagiarizing* or otherwise cheating as long as they come up with a "right answer" or the "right product"

Another significant characteristic of today's students is that few of them relish the prospect of visiting a library when they require assistance. Numerous studies have noted student *reluctance to approach librarians* for help. Typically, *they dislike being dependent* upon others for finding information when they need it, despite their acknowledged difficulties in finding reliable and accurate scholarly information.

Beyond the academy, Millennials are regarded as a powerful market force and are already exercising their muscles as consumers. The corporate world spends significant amounts of time and resources trying to better understand what motivates and appeals to young people in order to effectively market products and services to them. Customization is a key theme. When asked for their definitions of technology, Gen Y responds that it is *looking for something that adapts to their needs*, not something requiring them to change their habits. They call it "the ability to adapt and configure an already established program to [something that] benefits me daily," or alternately, "cutting-edge software that allows me to do what I want, when I want, without restrictions," or "the power to do what I need to do faster than the ancient methods of conducting things."[21] Although students continue to view expert faculty as a key ingredient for learning success, they identify the second most important support for learning as their professors' ability to *customize a class by using available technologies*. In the same way that Gen Y demands consumer products and services 24/7 in customized modes, so have they come to expect the same of university, instructional, and library services.

Recently, the information industry market research firm Outsell, Inc., explored the research and information-seeking habits of a select group of college students to determine whether research is a high priority for undergraduates, the extent to which they rely on libraries and faculty for guidance, and whether they are concerned with the quality of information they uncover. Based on its findings, Outsell believes that there currently exists a "window of opportunity" for the library to position itself at the center of the classroom and thus demonstrate its critical relevance to learning. As was the case with previous generations, Outsell found that *student use of libraries and sources is driven by the curriculum*. Students will mostly rely on course texts and required readings *unless* guided, encouraged, or required by faculty to explore the extensive learning support materials (including primary resources and scholarly sources) and learning pathways embodied in library collections, databases, and services.

Changing Paradigms in Teaching and Learning in Higher Education

> Today we live in a world in which … events occur in real time, effects are immediate, and reaction times are cut short. In many disciplines, the half-life of information is

measured in months ... From this perspective, what a person can do is more important than what degree they obtained.

Bill Gates[22]

At the 84th Annual Meeting of the American Council on Education, Anthony Carnevale, vice-president for public leadership at the Educational Testing Service, observed that most postsecondary education in the United States currently fails to focus on the skills that are necessary in today's rapidly changing world. He further suggested that *current economic forces demand fundamental changes in America's postsecondary curricula.* Alan E. Guskin and Mary B. Marcy second this opinion, noting, "In the next decade or so, increasingly severe financial and accountability pressures may well disrupt the educational and administrative practices of our nation's colleges and universities."[23] David E. Leveille, a scholar with the Center for Studies in Higher Education at the University of California, Berkeley, writes,

> The strength of the state's economy, the quality of its workforce, the vitality of its communities, and the productivity and well being of its citizens depend upon an education system that provides residents of all ages with the knowledge and skills needed to live, learn and work in a changing world.[24]

We know that Generation Y has a thirst for discovery-based learning and is comfortable learning and working in teams, a skill that will be required of them as they tackle the complex and interdisciplinary problems of the twenty-first century. And yet we also know from a variety of research that they often lack the critical thinking and evaluative skills that are critically important to scholarship and problem solving. Nancy Cantor of the State University of New York's Reinvention Center describes Gen Y, who in time will come to populate, manage, and lead in this changing world, *as needing to be educated* not *in facts,* but "in how to think," and to "operate from the premise that what they know now will be less true for tomorrow," and to "function in a society made up of many societies."[25] How might higher educators seek to prepare these students?

The Boyer Commission Report, *Reinventing Undergraduate Education,* which informed the development of the Information Literacy Competency Standards for Higher Education, foreshadowed much of today's discussion in higher education circles regarding the need for fundamental educational reform. It signaled a renewed interest in the philosophy of John Dewey, a leader of the progressive movement in American education, who suggested that deep learning results not from the *transmission* of information from faculty to students but, rather, from *independent discovery* carried out by students under the guidance of faculty mentors. The Boyer Commission observed, "Education by inquiry demands collaborative effort"[26] and described the university as a venue wherein ideas can be explored openly and developed productively through the collective engagement of faculty, graduate students, and undergraduates while building on the groundwork provided by preceding generations of scholars.

The commission proposed that scholar-teachers might even use their own research as an endeavor to which both undergraduates and graduate students also might contribute. Within this new model of higher education, the commission suggested that faculty time is best spent interacting with students and that faculty can learn from students at the same time that students are learning from them. It further noted that the "accidental collision of ideas" between faculty and students is a necessary factor not only in student engagement, but also in the continued productivity of faculty.

Moreover, the commission observed that students, as they engage in coursework with a variety of faculty, might serve as informal emissaries, breaking down some of the *false intellectual barriers* that exist among faculty and are reinforced by the current and traditional administrative structure of academic departments. The commission's observations and recommendations are reconfirmed in current higher education discussions, suggesting the need for the *restructuring of curricula*. The report anticipated that future work would require mental flexibility on the part of students and that, to prepare for this, current curricula must require students to *view their studies through a variety of disciplinary lenses*. It urged that serious focus be placed on creating *interdisciplinary learning experiences* for undergraduates. This dual focus on research-based learning and interdisciplinary learning, the commission contended, would require an *active collaboration* across departmental boundaries and among a variety of campus units.

The Boyer report went so far as to recommend that every course in the undergraduate curriculum be recast as research or discovery based. It also acknowledged the need for faculty to become more cognizant of their dual roles: first, in helping young scholars to frame meaningful research questions;

and second, in providing them with the tools they would need to explore "deeply as well as widely," to analyze and evaluate information, and to create scholarly products.

The more information a person can obtain, the greater the need for judgment about how to use it ... who teaches students how to take advantage of this mass of information? Who teaches them how to tell the difference between valuable information and clutter? How, in short, does a student become a more intelligent consumer in this supermarket of information?[27]

Although the report suggests that it is the scholar-teacher's responsibility to do so, with the advent of the Information Literacy Standards, it can be argued that librarians, too, have a significant role to play in this endeavor because libraries are organized to facilitate independent discovery and support interdisciplinary study.

Finally, the commission observed that, to fully comprehend course material as well as the research process in its entirety, students must be required to write and speak effectively and persuasively and demonstrate the ability to produce a scholarly work as a routine expectation of their undergraduate experience. Such an activity involves the higher-order thinking skills of analysis, synthesis, and evaluation delineated in the Information Literacy Standards and comprises elements of "critical thinking," a commonly agreed-upon learning goal of higher education. The 1998 Boyer report states,

All of the skills of research developed in earlier work should be marshaled in a project that demands the framing of a significant question or set of questions, the research or creative exploration to find answers, and the communication skills to convey the results to audiences both expert and uninitiated in the subject matter.[28]

This capstone project was envisioned as taking place within a small learning community made up of faculty experts, graduate students, and undergraduate peers. Subsequent discussions within higher education circles, in the United States and internationally, have suggested that this community encompass librarians, educational technologists, instructional designers, assessment experts, and other academic support personnel. The Boyer model assumes that all the participants within this learning community are both teachers and learners. The Boyer Commission concluded by urging American research universities to *enact necessary reforms to the curriculum* to achieve these goals. Libraries can play an active and vital role in contributing to the undergraduate's experience of higher education through the design of learning approaches and experiences requiring independent discovery, by drawing on the interdisciplinary strengths of library resources, and by implementing within course and curriculum design the Information Literacy Standards and outcomes that emphasize the development of analytical and evaluative skills in students.

If we fast-forward to twenty-first-century discussions about higher education reform, we see many of the same themes raised by the Boyer Commission Report revisited and reemphasized. In 2002, the Association of American Colleges and Universities (AACU) issued a report titled *Greater Expectations: A New Vision for Learning as a Nation Goes to College*. AACU describes the contemporary and complex environment of higher education wherein the answer to the question What is the role of a college education? differs, depending on which higher education stakeholders are asked. Students expect to be prepared to enter, advance in, and change careers. Faculty want students to be critical thinkers who can write well and *explore a wide range of academic fields*, and who remain committed to learning beyond the conferment of their baccalaureate degrees. Employers look for specific analytical, problem-solving, and information skills. Members of the public expect graduates to be able to succeed in their chosen careers and in their lives. Governments' and municipalities' interests lie in attracting businesses and industries, and they expect that, in order to do so, colleges and universities graduate students who are "information-ally" *and* technologically skilled. AACU observes that "higher education appears to be disengaged from many important social needs of contemporary society."[29] In its report, *What Work Requires of Schools:A SCANS Report for America 2000,* the U.S. Department of Labor's Commission on Achieving Necessary Skills called on America's schools, regardless of level, to transform themselves and *focus on a new set of competencies* encompassing resource management, interpersonal, systems, and information skills.

AACU contends that for the higher education community to succeed with education reforms, it must *define and support the types of learning* that today's students must master to function successfully within an increasingly complex world. The AACU panel proposes a "practical liberal education" as the solution to this challenge. Although, traditionally, the value of learning for learning's sake has been widely accepted within the academy, AACU has taken a step beyond, acknowledging a new role of U.S. higher education, one of *supporting practical knowledge and experiences* in creating the college or university educational experience. Although the curriculum of the past primarily involved the transmission of a body of knowledge, AACU recommends that the curriculum of the future focus instead on a well-informed, *student-enacted exploration of ideas and values.* In this way, graduates will be better prepared to meet a diverse and complex set of challenges facing society. In the same way that the Boyer report focused on the need for interdisciplinary research and education at the undergraduate level, the AACU report extends these emphases. Like the Boyer report in the late 1990s, drafters of the AACU report highlight the current and continuing explosion of available information and underscore the need for today's students to be able to find, evaluate, and use this information effectively.

AACU coined the phrase *empowered learner* to encompass a set of intellectual and practical skills that allows students to "understand and employ quantitative and qualitative analysis to solve problems, interpret and evaluate information from a variety of sources, transform information into knowledge and knowledge into judgment and action."[30] Student impressions serve to reinforce this point. Carie Windham, the student contributor to *Educating the Net Generation,* writes, "There is an unspoken sentiment within our ranks that the problems of the world have largely been deposited at our feet."[31] Similarly, in fall 2005, a small group of University of California, Berkeley, students, informally surveyed about the meaning they attach to a college education, frequently described it as the acquisition of knowledge *and* skills with the expressed purpose of applying them to the solution of real-world problems.

The *Greater Expectations* report describes the "responsible learner" as one possessing academic honesty. Considered together, learning goals that support the empowered learner and the responsible learner comprise the core of AACU's "practical liberal education." How does AACU propose the practical liberal education be realized in today's students? Like the Boyer report, AACU *identifies new roles required on the part of faculty.* AACU suggests that faculty, rather than functioning in relative isolation within their academic departments and being responsible primarily for the individual courses they teach, will need to *focus more generally on goals for student learning* within the context of a broader academic program and their institutions as a whole.

The traditional separation of general education requirements, requirements in the major, and electives has resulted in a fragmented curriculum. To reach the goal of producing empowered and responsible learners, AACU recommends integrating these three elements into a consistent whole to be delivered through a rich diversity of learning approaches. In this way, AACU anticipates meeting the need for high-level intellectual skills that emphasize adaptability and creative problem solving required by the workplace and the increasingly complex nature of problems facing contemporary society.

So, too, has the Higher Education Information Resources Alliance (HEIR), a group sponsored by the Association of Research Libraries and EDUCAUSE to keep higher education executives informed about critical planning issues, acknowledged that information and scholarship are changing and *challenged faculty to offer a more holistic view of learning* in place of tradition-bound subject specialties. In this way, faculty members can increase not only their connections, but also their students' connections, to other disciplines. This might be achieved by requiring students to approach their discovery-based learning through a multiplicity of disciplinary lenses, an activity the library is well situated to support. It also might be achieved by placing greater emphasis on the *integration of practical problem-solving skills,* such as information gathering, analysis, evaluation, and judgment, *within the curriculum.*

The AACU report suggests that the New Academy must support reforms in the curriculum and in teaching by the *strategic employment of campus resources.* It further suggests that curricular and cocurricular programs (such as general education courses, the library, freshmen experiences, and the like) can mutually reinforce one another and support the development of a student body comprising empowered and responsible learners. One interesting observation appearing in the AACU report relates to the preparation that scholars receive in assuming their roles as college and university teachers. "The dark secret of higher education is that most college professors are never trained as teachers."[32] AACU calls for "teaching and learning on every campus to make available significant resources to support faculty members as they assume the responsibilities of learning centered education."[33] Again, the library is well situated to support this discovery-based education by collaborating with faculty in the development of *research-based assignments* and by teaching students *practical information skills.* Like the Boyer Commission before it, the AACU panel recommends that college seniors "complete an integrative, capstone experience as evidence of advanced college-level learning."[34]

In his 2001 article in *Change* magazine, Ralph Mullin cites the curricular reform work conducted at Alverno College as a model for the effective integration of institution-wide learning goals. Alverno has enumerated eight abilities it feels best support students in becoming effective learners and establishes these abilities as *college-wide learning goals*. Counted among Alverno's "ability areas" are communication, analysis or critical thinking skills, and problem solving, which encompasses both problem definition and evaluation skills. A condition of graduation is the student's ability to demonstrate competence in the eight abilities. A well-developed performance assessment program serves as a replacement for course credits and grade point averages. Alverno's student-centered approach to higher learning holds great promise. An obvious connection can be drawn between Alverno's learning abilities and the Information Literacy Standards' performance indicators and learning outcomes.

Whether it be today's students, the Boyer Commission, the AACU, the U.S. Department of Labor, or other stakeholders in higher education, they have all identified the need for college and university curricula to address both the development of transferable, practical problem-solving skills (including information skills) and the placement of greater emphasis on interdisciplinary approaches to problem solving and learning. This will require more of campus faculty as they provide their students with the necessary tools to allow them to engage in independent, self-directed research and learning. It also serves as a call to libraries and other campus academic support units to share their knowledge and resources with faculty, providing them with needed support in meeting these new obligations. The Boyer Commission was quick to realize that the refocusing of college curricula on research-based and interdisciplinary study would require collaboration beyond the faculty ranks. Libraries can serve as vital partners in the development of both student information skills and interdisciplinary learning experiences for students.

Accountability in Higher Education

A third trend with implications for undergraduate research, information literacy, and instruction in library research skills is that of the increasingly visible and vocal accountability movement both inside and outside the walls of higher education. Increasingly, students, parents, legislators, accrediting agencies, and educational associations are calling for higher education to revise the way in which it measures its effectiveness and demonstrates its value. Faculty and institutions are being asked to define success in terms of the achievement of student learning outcomes and the cultivation of support structures and learning environments (including libraries) that support student-centered learning, student preparation, and student achievement. Leveille's article, "An Emerging View on Accountability in Higher Education," notes a number of concurrent conditions: increasing student tuition and fees and the public's concern over the rising costs; society's need for graduates well prepared to assume their roles and responsibilities in a complex world; and the demands from business and industry for employees possessing demonstrable analytical, problem-solving, and information skills.

It has been widely reported that the cost of higher education routinely outpaces America's Consumer Price Index and represents a greater share of most American family incomes than it did in preceding decades. Nancy Cantor of the State University of New York reports that for the decade ending in 1996, the average rise in net college tuition was 81 percent for private universities and 65 percent for public universities. Many higher education officials project that the cost of educating undergraduates will continue to grow with time and it is expected that an increased focus on accountability for student learning will as well.

The American Association of University Professors has noted a national concern among parents, students, and political leaders over their perception that the rising costs of higher education have failed to result in better educational outcomes for today's graduates. Those in elected office are demanding reassurances that public universities are making responsible use of public funds and delivering a high-quality educational experience at a reasonable cost. State Higher Education Executive Officers (SHEEO) consider accountability to be among the top three challenges to be met by public higher education.

David E. Leveille writes,

> Accountability is a public oriented process that seeks to assure public constituents of the value, effectiveness, and quality of higher education; it informs the public about institutional performance.[35]

AACU's proposal on accountability calls on its members to provide public statements of learning goals for all academic programs, along with credible documentation of the successful attainment of those goals. Forty-four states currently have formal accountability mandates. The remaining six an increase in agency requests for data on academic productivity. Twenty-one states use some form of performance measure when allocating educational funding and nearly all states tie performance indicators to part of their budget review. Leveille identifies three emerging trends in the accountability movement: a strong emphasis on educational results, a change from measuring inputs and processes to student performance as the key indicator of success, and a growing demand on the part of regional and professional accrediting bodies for evidence of student learning.

SHEEO has noted the public's priorities for higher education: better access and graduation rates, research beneficial to society at large, graduates capable of meeting critical labor needs, and improved student learning. It notes that these public priorities tend to take a back seat when colleges and universities compete for top spots among national rankings that are frequently based on institutional demographics (faculty reputation and student selectively), rather than on results, *the most important of which is student learning.*

SHEEO contends that in order for colleges and universities to demonstrate their value to society, professional associations, government, and accrediting bodies, the intense focus of accountability must be trained on the *realization of student learning.* Instead, the prevailing learning structure for undergraduate education is based on the course credit system, developed in the late nineteenth century to measure institutional efficiency. It has persisted over time because it is easy to measure, yet it tells institutions little or nothing about their success in improving student learning, students' abilities to successfully demonstrate needed practical skills, or problem solvers' abilities to make conceptual connections across disciplines. Twentieth-century performance indicators included the test ranks and grade point averages of incoming students, number of degrees awarded, graduation rates, enrollments in a major, and student–faculty ratios.

Accountability of the kind currently practiced, SHEEO contends, does not result in improved institutional performance. SHEEO recommends, instead, that *institutional learning goals* be defined for all academic programs by university leaders and trustees that are consistent with public priorities, assessable, and unequivocally communicated to students. SHEEO further recommends the appropriate venue for the assessment of student learning is within institutions because it will directly influence faculty and students who do the work and allow institutions who fail to meet their goals to take remedial action. Institutions, faculty, and students must be aware of learning performance standards, student progress must be measured against institutional learning goals and standards, and everyone concerned must continually work to improve student learning. To do so will require the development of faculty skills in the design of formative and summative assessment and rubrics.

Beyond institutional goal setting and assessment, SHEEO also recommends that accrediting associations set learning goals appropriate to the conferment of particular degrees and assess institutional performance against established standards. Six regional higher education accreditation associations have increasingly pressured colleges and universities to assess their attainment of student learning outcomes as part of the accreditation review. The Western Association of Schools and Colleges (WASC) has developed a specific criteria set for accreditation, working to improve the gathering of evidence of teaching effectiveness and student learning. Of particular interest to libraries is the WASC guideline stating, "The use of information and learning resources beyond textbooks is evidenced in syllabi throughout the undergraduate and graduate curriculum."[36] Like the Boyer and AACU reports, SHEEO underscores the need for universities to realize significant progress toward successful student learning and that to do so, they will have to change. Faculty will have to provide leadership in designing more coherent academic programs that result in the graduation of "empowered, responsible learners" and in developing more authentic assessments of student learning to support achievement of this critical aspiration.

AACU expresses a similar set of recommendations by calling for faculty to set clear, interrelated, and integrated learning goals for individual courses and for programs of instruction while articulating standards for the achievement of these goals. It calls for the development of a *culture of evidence* within the New Academy, which itself becomes a necessary support to greater student achievement and which results in improved campus curricula, teaching, and learning. AACU believes the central question in higher education is simple, albeit complex: What types of learning should result from an undergraduate education? By focussing on a common set of student learning outcomes, Joseph Brewer contends that colleges and universities can begin to recognize and assess learning, regardless of where that learning takes place (whether through independent or online study, as a consequence of library research, during internships, or through other learning experiences).

In setting standards for the acquisition of skills and knowledge required to solve complex and interdisciplinary problems, AACU suggests that colleges and universities can better demonstrate their value to society and the extent to which their students possess the practical, analytical, and intellectual skills and evaluative judgment that a baccalaureate degree should represent. With a renewed emphasis on learning, the development of the learner assumes greater importance than the subject matter taught, the credit hours earned, or the number of classes completed. SHEEO's and AACU's recommended action steps are the same: universities must set explicit goals and expectations for student learning across the undergraduate curriculum, design purposeful learning pathways that incorporate both general education and disciplinary studies, and align assessment efforts in such a way that they measure student progress toward and achievement of these goals.

With the proper structures in place and a commitment to collaboration and outreach, libraries can play an instrumental role in helping faculty and institutions to demonstrate institutional effectiveness by defining student learning outcomes around the transferable skills of interdisciplinary information exploration, analysis, and evaluation and at the same time meet the expectations of students, future employers, accrediting agencies, and professional associations. The Information Literacy Standards provide an useful jumping-off place from which librarians can begin their work with faculty to integrate information literacy learning goals and outcomes as appropriate into a course, a program, or an institution's stated learning goals for all undergraduates.

The National Center for Public Policy and Higher Education is exploring alternative strategies for assessing the effectiveness of higher educational institutions. The center publishes a biennial report titled *Measuring Up: The National Report Card on Higher Education*. *Measuring Up* has constructed a series of measurement categories, including a "learning" category, that attempt to measure such things as the abilities and performance of the college educated population and the institutional contributions to this educational capital. It creates a learning profile for each of the fifty states as a way of stimulating public policies that will improve the accessibility and effectiveness of higher education. To date, the center has been unable to grade the states on the sixth comparison category, the "learning" category, because of the lack of available and comparable data across states. As a result, in conjunction with the *Measuring Up* initiative, the states of Illinois, Kentucky, Nevada,

Oklahoma, and North Carolina have developed a set of learning measures for a national demonstration project funded by The Pew Charitable Trust to compare learning results across states. Regardless of the approach taken, Leveille suggests that the *key higher education performance indicators* for the twenty-first century must include: personal attention from faculty/mentors, access to a global information network and unlimited library collections, a flexible curriculum, personalized learning systems, demonstrable value of the educational program, and lifelong learning support. These are all areas in which the library can play a critical, indeed, a leadership role.

The University of California, Berkeley, Experience

Many within the higher education community are calling on faculty to assume new roles and responsibilities for the design of student-centered liberal education programs with particular emphasis on interdisciplinary problem solving and the development of transferable skills. Some have noted how faculty often are not trained as teachers and therefore require significant institutional support to meet these changing expectations. Closing the gaps between curricular (faculty) and cocurricular (library, general education, freshmen experience, etc.) programs while working with other academic support units (educational technology and teaching centers) can be an effective means of supporting faculty as they move in needed, new directions to restructure courses and curricula that support independent discovery and self-directed learning.

In his article "Libraries Dealing with the Future Now," Joseph Brewer describes the "transformed library" as one that "provides ... for inquiry based learning and out of classroom activities" and "develops new and innovative learning environments and activities through collaboration with other academic units."[37] Included among Brewer's principles underlying the transformed library are the following: the library collaboratively creates learning environments that allow faculty to teach in new and more discovery-based ways; the responsibilities for instruction in library research and information skills are shared by the entire campus; and librarians spend more time partnering in course and curriculum design and less time engaged in the delivery of individual course instructional sessions. The transformed library, then, becomes a key factor to faculty success as they address the many challenges introduced by the Boyer report, the accountability movement, the American Association of Colleges and Universities, Generation Y, and others.

The Library at the University of California, Berkeley, is trying to become that transformed library. Berkeley's recent Accreditation Educational Effectiveness Report identified several challenges to the campus in scaling the research-based undergraduate education so strongly urged by the Boyer report and others. In particular, Berkeley noted inadequate research and writing skills possessed by undergraduates who are required to complete a capstone project, a finding that has been mirrored elsewhere in the self-reports of Generation Y's, and in faculty and librarian observations. The Berkeley accreditation report also noted the absence of a campus assessment program to monitor the progress of undergraduates engaged in research and how research-based assignments and activities contribute to their learning.

At Berkeley, as elsewhere, higher education administrators and faculty are increasingly being required by a variety of stakeholders to demonstrate their value and effectiveness. In addition to research distinction, that value is defined in terms of student learning. Professional and accrediting bodies have repeatedly called on universities to articulate clear, interrelated, and integrated institutional learning goals and to establish measures, standards, and tools for assessing their success in reaching these goals. What the Berkeley campus *did* know as a result of its 2002 and 2003 Undergraduate Experience Survey is this: 95 percent of graduating seniors rated the development of research skills as an important educational goal, yet only 44 percent reported having made considerable progress toward this goal. Eighty-six percent said that obtaining knowledge and skills required for their careers was "essential" or "very important." Ninety percent considered conducting their own research as part of a course "very important," and 77 percent considered independent study "important." Less than half had engaged in the latter.

Since 2002, the University Library at Berkeley has been working to address all these concerns. Library staff initiated a campuswide conversation with other academic support units interested in the development of interactive, research-based, and technologically facilitated learning experiences for undergraduates. Staff from the Division of Undergraduate Education, Educational Technological Services, Graduate Student Instructor Training and Resource Center, and the Office of Educational Development initially joined the University Library to form the Academic Partners group. The Academic Partners drafted pilot and follow-on funding proposals, grounded in the development of a long-term, sustainable campus collaboration, the aim of which was to share skills and leverage resources to promote and realize the redesign of undergraduate courses and curricula that emphasize the development of library-based undergraduate research skills. The Academic Partners realized that a scalable model for developing undergraduate research skills and discovery-based learning on the campus must begin with campus faculty members who oversee the curriculum and are the primary agents of curriculum reform on the campus.

The collaborative infrastructure being developed by the Academic Partners supports faculty interested in these new ways of undergraduate teaching, ways that incorporate library research skills and the ability to analyze, evaluate, and use information ethically as key learning goals of the courses they design and teach. Redesigned courses might employ technological solutions to teaching and learning, when appropriate, and selectively introduce classroom assessment techniques and the assessment of student learning resulting from research-based assignments and activities.

With support from the Andrew W. Mellon Foundation, the Academic Partners began their work by designing the Mellon Library/Faculty Fellowship on Undergraduate Research Institute. Offered each summer, the six-day institute is designed to model active learning and assessment strategies through the use of in-class activities, discussions, written reflections, media, as well as a range of assessment methods. Faculty are selected as fellows discuss a range of topics related to developing effective undergraduate research-based syllabi and assignments. They are invited to write learning outcomes for their courses and to design assignments that will challenge undergraduates to use the library's print and digital resources and engage in the process of scholarly discovery.

Priority in the selection process is given to faculty who teach large-enrollment, lower-division courses, particularly courses required for a major. In this way, the Academic Partners intend to address a priority articulated in Berkeley's Western Association of Schools and Colleges Educational Effectiveness Report, that of providing research-based learning and foundation skills development for all lower-division students. It is also hoped that by focusing on large-enrollment courses and courses required in a major that the faculty and Academic Partners will be able to affect the learning of large numbers of undergraduates on the campus.

By the end of the four-year Mellon Library/Faculty Fellowship for Undergraduate Research Project, four cohorts of nine to fourteen faculty members each from a wide range of disciplines will have participated in a series of activities beginning with the annual Mellon Library/Faculty Institute.

Following the institute, Mellon fellows are each partnered with an Implementation Team (iTeam) made up of librarians, instructional technology experts, pedagogy experts, and other academic support staff. The teams work with faculty to refine syllabi and assignments, and integrate technology and assessment into course development where appropriate. Each year, several fellows are invited to participate in a range of assessment strategies that allow them to measure how the changes they have made to their courses have affected their students' learning.

In addition to receiving a stipend, fellows may submit post-institute proposals for additional funding. Collections funds provided by the library may be used to acquire or digitize materials in support of Mellon-related courses. Educational technology funds provided through the Mellon project can be used to purchase educational technologies and/or to contract for educational technology services. Innovation funds, also provided by the project, may be used to support scaleable and sustainable changes to the curriculum, departmental implementations, and teaching tools that incorporate information competencies, research skills, and the use of campus information resources as integral components, or to assess the impact of research assignments on student learning and faculty teaching.

One means of maintaining the collaborations formed during the institute and building new collaborations among the cohorts from year to year, as well as between the fellows and the Academic Partners and their staffs, takes the form of a series of semiannual salons to which the fellows, Academic Partners, and Implementation Team members are invited. The salons serve to develop this community, dedicated to leveraging the university' research strength to enhance undergraduate education, and to nurture the Mellon faculty in their roles as agents of change within the teaching culture of the university. In these ways, the Berkeley Library aims to initiate campuswide changes in the curriculum and support the faculty in their emerging responsibilities for student-centered and discovery-based learning. The changes that are realized in the curriculum equally serve to respond to the learning preferences and habits of Generation Y and to the demands for greater accountability within the higher education community.

Higher Education Trends and Their Implications for Libraries

The preceding trends have significant implications for information literacy and undergraduate research instruction librarians, not only in terms of what and how they teach, but also in the products and services they develop and in how they function within the larger teaching and learning communities on their campuses. Stanley M. Davis, futurist and author of *Blur: The Speed of Change in the Connected Economy*, pinpoints competition to attract the attention of the individual as one of the most challenging issues of the twenty-first century.

If libraries are to attract the attention of Gen Y, what do these trends in student behaviors and learning styles signify for instruction librarians? Clearly, libraries will have to meet Generation Y in the real and virtual places they inhabit and by designing learning and information access systems that meet Gen Y's preferences for networked resources, speed, interactivity, and customization, while at the same time supporting their desire for self-sufficiency and inclination toward "bricolage." Joan Lippincott notes that as more and more faculty employ learning management and course management systems, libraries will need to make themselves more visible within these, rather than expecting students to visit the library's home page to access information and materials they need for their courses (or to attend drop-in instructional sessions to learn how).

We know that the expectations and learning habits of today's students differ significantly from previous generations, and the world in which Gen Y, the faculty, and librarians inhabit is rapidly changing, too. Diana Oblinger observes that many of the attributes of interactive games also make for good student learning environments: they allow players to pose questions, explore, make decisions, and problem solve. Lippincott urges libraries to explore more visually oriented learning tools as a response to Gen Y's multimedia orientation. These observations, in part, address the student engagement needs of Millennials. The University of Virginia's interactive Web site, The Valley of the Shadow, which allows students to explore and analyze online primary resources through multiple paths and to draw their own conclusions about the Civil War, is one example of such a resource.

In our larger society and in the business world in particular, there is a clear move taking place away from mass marketing and production to mass customization. This is what Millennials have come to expect and libraries would do well to focus less on marketing standardized instruction and tools and more on exploring ways of customizing learning tools and environments for Millennials who engage in library research instruction.

Both students and faculty have expressed doubts about students' abilities to find scholarly materials appropriate to their research and study, to analyze and evaluate information and resources, and to understand the conventions of scholarly communication. Clearly, these areas will need to assume greater importance in library research instruction in the future rather than the features and mechanics of individual databases or the particulars of searching a given resource. Millennials need and want less focus on facts and information and greater emphasis on approaches and skills that are transferable across databases, sources, and projects. This is yet another strategy that libraries can employ to attract the attention of Generation Y.

Both universities and libraries must consider a range of instructional strategies to meet student learning goals, including technology-based products and services, learning communities, peer learning, in-class activities, and individual learning. If the growing trend in nontraditional students persists, and if the information economy continues to require workers to engage in ongoing education, remote and distributed access to library-based learning tools will allow students to make better use of their time, engage them when they are "learning ready," and reduce the hours they might otherwise spend commuting to and from campus.

We know that Generation Ys are constant communicators, accustomed to teamwork, and focused on activities that lead to "a grade." This implies that library research instruction needs to provide opportunities for student interaction and group work and, more important, that it needs to be embedded within courses and in the curriculum requirements articulated by the faculty. This speaks to the need for librarians to attract the attention of faculty on their campuses.

In a paper prepared for the Association of Research Libraries, Kenneth Smith, Distinguished Service Professor at the University of Arizona, noted that for libraries to prosper in the twenty-first century, they will have to better understand the pressures and the changing expectations faced by universities and develop approaches that allow libraries to place themselves at the center of their universities' response to these challenges. Smith asks, What is the relationship between the academic program, the curriculum, and the co-curriculum (including libraries) in meeting particular student learning goals and outcomes? He observes that libraries have traditionally focused on making greater amounts of information accessible rather than on how they might influence and directly address learning outcomes that are critical to student success. Further, he cites the work of the American Association of Higher Education, which concludes that the assessment of student learning cannot be addressed adequately without the contributions of libraries and other cocurricular units. An economist, Smith contends that the "value added" provided by libraries will increasingly need to involve how they, as learning organizations, contribute to the achievement of institutional learning goals. This will require instruction librarians to learn more about course and curriculum design and methodologies in order to serve as knowledgeable supports to the faculty in the roles they are now expected to perform.

Information literacy learning outcomes can serve as institutional learning outcomes, as they involve critical thinking, analysis, evaluation, and communication skills, the need for which spans the range of campus academic programs. Serving to support this argument is a National Research Council report, *Being Fluent in Information Technology,* which incorporates both information technology and information literacy skills as a single skill set, something currently referred to by many in the library community as "information fluency." The report recommends that each of the university's subject areas and programs develop ways to incorporate information instruction into the curriculum while noting that this is currently not the case at most universities.

The concept of undergraduate research and its attendant information literacy skills can serve as a fulcrum to support the idea of the library as a relevant and appropriate partner in meeting the campus's teaching mission and in supporting students' independent, self-directed learning. An analysis of College Student Experiences Questionnaire (CSEQ) data underscores the critical need for libraries to partner with faculty and other student learning professionals to ensure that learning objectives for information literacy and undergraduate research are factored into the design of courses and programs of instruction. Equally important is the need for students to receive a consistent and clear message regarding the value of learning about and using scholarly information resources and for faculty to require evidence that students are making appropriate judgments about the credibility and value of the information they are using to learn.

In an article about the hidden assumptions that faculty make about their students' skills in conducting research, Gloria J. Leckie focuses on the need for librarians to

> concentrate on developing their working relationships with
> faculty, fostering an environment where the skills and knowledge

of both groups can be harmonized to better benefit students and enhance the institution.[38]

Instruction librarians also can add value by being more proactive in identifying and promoting collections of learning objects and digital materials that faculty can use in instruction.

Conclusion

In a presentation titled "The Role of the Academic Library in Promoting Student Engagement in Learning," George D. Kuh observed that libraries can play an important role in helping institutions to achieve their academic missions. The Association of American Colleges and Universities (AACU) asserts that intellectual growth takes place when broad and deep learning *challenges* previously held beliefs. Libraries, and library instruction librarians in particular, can play a critical role in challenging students to independently explore a wide range of divergent views on nearly any topic imaginable and by providing them with the intellectual and practical skills to engage in this type of scholarly and practical inquiry. In the words of one University of California, Berkeley, student enrolled in a research-based course:

> The way the course was undertaken, with us being allowed to undertake research that really gave life to the history material, shapes the way I perceive American history now ... the credibility that I grant things ... I now approach them in a very analytical way, I would like to think ... I would feel compelled to research beneath and beyond what I am being told.[39]

A number of higher education associations, committees, and think tanks are changing their notions of what constitutes a liberal education. They now feel it depends not so much on the mastery of a particular body of subject knowledge but, instead, on an approach to teaching and learning that focuses on the development of transferable student skills and interdisciplinary competencies. A primary goal of higher education must be to provide students not only with discrete knowledge, but also with the information, analytic, and evaluative skills they will need to continue to learn over the course of a lifetime. Leckie has written,

There must be a convergence of both information and
disciplinary literacy if true learning is to be facilitated, therefore,
both librarians and faculty have to be involved in this process
together.[40]

Academic departments are now being required by higher education
stakeholders to prepare students in ways that call for the expertise of those
outside their fields. This need creates a window of opportunity for instruction
librarians. Will departmental faculty identify the library as a locus of help?
Perhaps not. Instruction librarians must seize this unique opportunity to
position themselves near the center of course and curriculum development and
assessment planning, and thus become a central support to the educational
mission of their universities. In the same way it takes a village to raise a child,
it takes an entire campus to produce a liberally educated undergraduate.

Notes

1. *Bears in the Library: Cal Students Talk about Research*, VHS, produced and
directed by Patricia Davitt Maughan (Regents of the University of California, 2004).
Available online from http://teles.berkeley.edu:8080/ramgen/2002/special_events/
lib/mellonresearch.rm. [Accessed 9 December 2005].

2. Karen Hein, "President's Essay: The Millenium and Millennials Unfolding" (New
York: William T. Grant Foundation, Apr. 2001), 2. Available online from http://www.
wtgrantfoundation.org/usr_doc/Karens%20essay.pdf. [Accessed 10 January 2005].

3. Diana Oblinger, "Boomers, Gen-Xers & Millennials: Understanding the New
Students," *EDUCAUSE Review* (July/Aug. 2003): 39. Available online from http://
www.educause.edu/ir/library/pdf/erm0342.pdf. [Accessed 10 January 2006].

4. Laura Randall, "The Gadgets They've Got and Why They've Got Them," *New York
Times*, 3 August 2005, Special Section E, The Digital Student, E4–5. Available online from
http://www.nytimes.com/2005/08/03/technology/techspecial3/03randall.html?
pagewanted=2&ei=5070. [Accessed 14 March 2006].

5. Ibid.

6. Hein, "President's Essay," 2.

7. Neil Howe and William Strauss, *Millennials Go to College*, (n.p.: LifeCourse
Associates and the American Association of Collegiate Registrars and Admissions
Officers, 2003). Available online from http://www.lifecourse.com/college. [Accessed
9 December 2005].

8. Ibid.

9. Carie Windham, "The Student's Perspective," in *Educating the Net Generation*, ed. Diana G. Oblinger and James L. Oblinger (Washington, DC: Educause, 2005), 5.3. Available online from http://www.educause.edu/educatingthenetgen. [Accessed 5 December 2005].

10. Ibid., 5.7.

11. Roberta Furger, "High School Goes High Tech," *PARADE Magazine* (Aug. 7, 2005): 14. Available online from http://www.parade.com/articles/editions/2005/edition_08-07-2005/featured_2. [Accessed 9 January 2006].

12. Windham, "The Student's Perspective," 5.12.

13. Ibid., 5.8.

14. Jason L. Frand, "The Information Mindset: Changes in Students and the Implications for Higher Education," *EDUCAUSE review* 35, no. 5 (Sept./Oct. 2000): 17. Available online from http://www.educause.edu/apps/er/erm00/articles005/erm0051.pdf. [Accessed 9 January 2006].

15. Mark Prensky, "Digital Natives, Digital Immigrants, Part II: Do They Really Think Differently?" *On the Horizon*, vol. 9, no. 6 (December 2001), 15–24. Available from http://www.marcprensky.com/writing/. Reprinted in part from William D. Winnn, Human Interface Technology Laboratory, University of Washington, quoted in Peter Moore, "Inferential Focus Briefing," September 30, 1997.

16. *Bears in the Library*.

17. Oblinger, "Boomers, Gen-Xers & Millennials," 40.

18. Joan K. Lippincott, "Net Generation Students and Libraries," in *Educating the Net Generation*, ed. Diana G. Oblinger and James L. Oblinger (Washington, DC: Educause, 2005),. Available online from http://www.educause.edu/NetGenerationStudentsandLibraries/6067. [Accessed 5 December 2005].

19. Howe and Strauss, *Millennials Go to College*.

20. Outsell, Inc., "Today's Students, Tomorrow's FGUs," *Information about Information Briefings* 3, no. 24 (Oct. 16, 2000): 3.

21. Gregory R. Roberts, "Technology and Learning Expectations of the Net Generation," in *Educating the Net Generation*, ed. Diana G. Oblinger and James L. Oblinger (Washington, DC: Educause, 2005), 3.2. Available online from http://www.educause.edu/TechnologyandLearningExpectationsoftheNetGeneration/6056. [Accessed 5 December 2005].

22. Bill Gates quoted in Frand, "The Information Mindset," 17.

23. Alan E. Guskin and Mary B. Marcy, "Pressures for Fundamental Reform: Creating a Viable Academic Future," in *Field Guide to Academic Leadership*, ed. Robert M. Diamond (San Francisco: Jossey-Bass, 2002), 4.

24. David E. Leveille, "An Emerging View on Accountability in American Higher Education," University of California, Berkeley. Center for Studies in Higher Education Research & Occasional Paper Series CSHE.8.05 (May 2005). Available online from http://repositories.cdlib.org/cshe/CSHE-8-05/. [Accessed 6 December 2005].

24. Nancy Cantor, "Reinvention: Why now? Why us? A Second Anniversary Retrospective on the Boyer Commission Report." Remarks by Provost Nancy Cantor, University of Michigan, April 28, 2000. Available online from http://www.sunysb.edu/Reinventioncenter/Cantor%20talk.htm. [Accessed 5 September 2002].

25. The Boyer Commission on Educating Undergraduates in the Research University, *Reinventing Undergraduate Education: A Blueprint for America's Research Universities* (Stoneybrook: State University of New York, 1998), 16. Available online from http://naples.cc.sunysb.edu/Pres/boyer.nsf/. [Accessed 6 December 2005].

26. Ibid., 26.

27. Ibid., 27.

28. Greater Expectations National Panel, Association of Colleges and Universities, *Greater Expectations: A New Vision for Learning as a Nation Goes to College* (Washington, DC: Association of American Colleges and Universities, 2002), 8. Available online from http://www.greaterexpectations.org. [Accessed 9 January 2006].

29. Ibid.

30. Windham, "The Student's Perspective," 5.5.

31. Greater Expectations National Panel, *Greater Expectations*, 16.

32. Ibid., 50.

33. Ibid., 49.

34. Leveille, "An Emerging View on Accountability in American Higher Education," 3.

36. Western Association of Schools and Colleges, *WASC Handbook of Accreditation*. 2001 (Alameda, CA: Western Association of Schools and Colleges, 2001), 21. Available online from http://education.berkeley.edu/accreditation/pdf/WASC_Handbook.pdf. [Accessed 5 December 2005].

37. Joseph M. Brewer et al., "Libraries Dealing with the Future Now," *ARL Bimonthly Report* 234 (June 2004). Available online from http://www.arl.org/newsltr/234/dealing.html. [Accessed 9 January 2006].

38. Gloria J. Leckie, "Desperately Seeking Citations: Uncovering Faculty Assumptions about the Undergraduate Research Process," *Journal of Academic Librarianship* 22, no. 3 (May 1996): 207.

39. *Bears in the Library.*

40. Leckie, "Desperately Seeking Citations," 206.

Bibliography

American Library Association, *Libraries, Literacy & Learning in the 21st Century* (Chicago: ALA, n.d.).

Ayers, Edward L., *The Valley of the Shadow* (Charlottesville, VA: Virginia Center for Digital History, University of Virginia: c1993–2006). Available online from http://valley.vcdh.virginia.edu/. [Accessed 6 December 2005].

Bears in the Library: Cal Students Talk about Research, produced and directed by Patricia Davitt Maughan. VHS (Regents of the University of California, 2004). Available online from http://teles.berkeley.edu:8080/ramgen/2002/special_events/lib/mellonresearch.rm. [Accessed 9 December 2005].

Benton Foundation, *Buildings, Books, and Bytes* (Washington, DC: Benton Foundation, 1996). Available online from http://www.benton.org/publibrary/kellogg/buildings.html. [Accessed 13 January 2006].

Best Practices Initiative, Institute for Information Literacy, Association of College and Research Libraries, "Characteristics of Programs of Information Literacy that Illustrate Best Practices: A Guideline." Available online from http://www.ala.org/ala/acrl/acrlstandards/characteristics.htm. [Accessed 9 January 2006].

The Boyer Commission on Educating Undergraduates in the Research University, *Reinventing Undergraduate Education: A Blueprint for America's Research Universities* (Stonybrook, NY: State University of New York, 1998). Available online from http://naples.cc.sunysb.edu/Pres/boyer.nsf/. [Accessed 6 December 2005].

Brewer, Joseph M., and others, "Libraries Dealing with the Future Now," *ARL Bimonthly Report* 234 (June 2004). Available online from http://www.arl.org/newsltr/234/dealing.html. [Accessed 9 January 2006].

Brown, John Seely, "Growing Up Digital: How the Web Changes Work, Education, and the Ways People Learn," *Change* (Mar./Apr. 2000): 11–20.

Cantor, Nancy, "Reinvention: Why now? Why us? A Second Anniversary Retrospective on the Boyer Commission Report" (remarks by Provost Nancy Cantor, University of Michigan, Apr. 28, 2000). Available online from http://www.sunysb.edu/Reinventioncenter/Cantor%20talk.htm. [Accessed 5 September 2002].

Chickering, Arthur W., and Stephen C. Ehrmann, "Implementing the Seven Principles: Technology as Lever." Available online from http://www.tltgroup.org/programs/seven.html. [Accessed 9 January 2006].

Cooperative Institutional Research Program, University of California, Los Angeles, "CIRP Freshman Survey." Available online from http://www.gseis.ucla.edu/heri/freshman.html. [Accessed 10 January 2006].

Davis, Stanley M., and Christopher Meyer, *Blur: The Speed of Change in the Connected Economy* (Reading, MA: Addison Wesley, 1998).

"Demographic Shifts Impact Higher Education Panel Says," *American Council on Education E 84th Annual Meeting Highlights* 51, no.4 (Mar. 4, 2002). Available online from http://192.111.222.22/hena/issues/2002/03-04-02/am.demographics.cfm. [Accessed 9 January 2006].

Frand, Jason L., "The Information Mindset: Changes in Students and the Implications for Higher Education," *EDUCAUSE review* 35, no. 5 (Sept./Oct. 2000): 15–24. Available online from http://www.educause.edu/apps/er/erm00/articles005/erm0051.pdf. [Accessed 9 January 2006].

Furger, Roberta, "High School Goes High Tech," *PARADE Magazine* (Aug. 7, 2005): 14–15. Available online from http://www.parade.com/articles/editions/2005/edition_08-07-2005/featured_2. [Accessed 9 January 2006].

Greater Expectations National Panel, Association of Colleges and Universities, *Greater Expectations: A New Vision for Learning as a Nation Goes to College* (Washington, DC: Association of American Colleges and Universities, 2002). Available online from http://www.greaterexpectations.org. [Accessed 9 January 2006].

Guskin, Alan G., and Mary B. Marcy, "Facing the Future: Faculty Work, Student Learning, and Fundamental Reform," Working Paper no.1, Project on the Future of Higher Education (Dec. 2001). Available online from http://www.pfhe.org/docs/PFHE.WP1.pdf. [Accessed 9 January 2006].

———, "Pressures for Fundamental Reform: Creating a Viable Academic Future," in *Field Guide to Academic Leadership*, ed. Robert M. Diamond (San Francisco: Jossey-Bass, 2002), 3–14.

Hartman, Joel, Patsy Moskal, and Chuck Dziuban, "Preparing the Academy of Today for the Learner of Tomorrow," in *Educating the Net Generation*, ed. Diana G. Oblinger and James L. Oblinger (Washington, DC: Educause, 2005), 6.1–6.14. Available online from http://www.educause.edu/educatingthenetgen.

Hein, Karen, "President's Essay: The Millenium and Millennials Unfolding" (New York: William T. Grant Foundation, April 2001). Available online from http://www.wtgrantfoundation.org/usr_doc/Karens%20essay.pdf. [Accessed 10 January 2005].

Higher Education Information Resources Alliance. "Executive Outlook on…the Transformation of Higher Education," HEIRAlliance Executive Strategies

Report (July 1996). Available online from http://www.educause.edu/ir/library. html/heir/hei1070.html. [Accessed 10 January 2006].

Howe, Neil, and William Strauss, *Millennials Go to College* (n.p.: LifeCourse Associates and the American Association of Collegiate Registrars and Admissions Officers, 2003). Available online from http://www.lifecourse.com/college. [Accessed 9 December 2005].

Hughes, Carol Ann, "Information Services for Higher Education," *D-Lib Magazine* 6, no. 12 (Dec. 2000). Available online from http://www.dlib.org/dlib/december00/ hughes/12hughes.html. [Accessed 9 January 2006].

Jones, Steve, "The Internet Goes to College: How Students Are Living in the Future with Today's Technology" (Washington, DC: Pew Internet & American Life Project, 2002). Available online from http://www.pewinternet.org/PPF/r/71/ report_display.asp. [Accessed 10 January 2006].

Kuh, George D., "Assessing What Really Matters to Student Learning," *Change* 33, no. 3 (May 1, 2001). Available online from http://www.pewtrusts.com/news/ news_subpage.cfm?content_item_id=540&content_type_id=13&page=nr2. [Accessed 10 January 2005].

Kuh, George D., and Robert M. Gonyea, "The Role of the Academic Library in Promoting Student Engagement in Learning" (paper presented at the 11th National Conference of the Association of College and Research Libraries, Charlotte, North Carolina, Apr. 10–13, 2003). Available online from http:// www.ala.org/ala/acrl/acrlevents/kuh.pdf. [Accessed 9 January 2006].

Leckie, Gloria J., "Desperately Seeking Citations: Uncovering Faculty Assumptions about the Undergraduate Research Process," *Journal of Academic Librarianship* 22, no. 3 (May 1996): 201–8.

Lenhart, Amanda, et al. "Teenage Life Online: The Rise of the Instant-message Generation and the Internet's Impact on Friendships and Family Relationships" (Washington, DC: Pew Internet & American Life Project, June 21, 2001). Available online from http://www.pewinternet.org/pdfs/PIP_Teens_Report.pdf. [Accessed 10 January 2006].

Leveille, David E., "An Emerging View on Accountability in American Higher Education," University of California, Berkeley. Center for Studies in Higher Education Research & Occasional Paper Series CSHE.8.05 (May 2005). Available online from http://repositories.cdlib.org/cshe/CSHE-8-05/. [Accessed 6 December 2005].

Lippincott, Joan K., "Net Generation Students and Libraries," in *Educating the Net Generation*, ed. Diana G. Oblinger and James L. Oblinger (Washington, DC:

Educause, 2005), 13.1–13.15. Available online from http://www.educause.edu/ NetGenerationStudentsandLibraries/6067. [Accessed 5 December 2005].

————, "Where Learners Go: How to Strengthen the Library Role in Online Teaching," *Library Journal* 130, no. 16 (Oct. 1, 2005): 35–37.

Lynch, Beverly, and others, "The Centrality of the Library: Views of Presidents and Provosts" (presentation at the 12th national conference of the Association of College and Research Libraries, Minneapolis, April 8, 2005).

Merrow, John, *Declining by Degrees* (Stanford, CA: Carnegie Foundation for the Advancement of Teaching, May 2005). Available online from http://www. carnegiefoundation.org/perspectives/perspectives2005.May.htm. [Accessed 6 December 2005].

————, "Survival of the Fittest," *New York Times* (Late Edition, East Coast) 24 April 2005, A:21: 4.

Mullin, Ralph, "The Undergraduate Revolution: Change the System or Give Incrementalism Another 30 Years?" *Change* 33, no.5 (Sept./Oct. 2001): 54–58.

National Center for Public Policy and Higher Education, "Measuring Up 2004: The National Report Card on Higher Education" (San Jose, CA: National Center for Public Policy and Higher Education, n.d.). Available online from http:// measuringup.highereducation.org/default.cfm. [Accessed 6 December 2005].

National Commission on Accountability in Higher Education, "Accountability for Better Results: A National Imperative on Accountability in Higher Education" (Boulder, CO: State Higher Education Executive Officers, 2005). Available online from http://www.sheeo.org/account/accountability.pdf. [Accessed 10 January 2006].

Oblinger, Diana, "Boomers, Gen-Xers & Millennials: Understanding the New Students," *EDUCAUSE review* (July/Aug. 2003): 37–47. Available online from http://www.educause.edu/ir/library/pdf/erm0342.pdf. [Accessed 10 January 2006].

Oblinger, Diana, and James Oblinger, "Is It Age or IT: First Steps toward Understanding the Net Generation," in *Educating the Net Generation*, ed. Diana G. Oblinger and James L. Oblinger (Washington, DC: Educause, 2005), 2.1–2.20. Available online from http://www.educause.edu/IsItAgeorIT:FirstSteepsTowardUndersta ndingtheNetGeneration/6058. [Accessed 5 December 2005].

Outsell, Inc., "Today's Students, Tomorrow's FGUs," *Information about Information Briefings* 3, no. 24 (Oct. 16, 2000).

Randall, Laura, "The Gadgets They've Got and Why They've Got Them," *New York Times* (3 August 2005), Special Section E, The Digital Student, E4–5. Available online

from http://www.nytimes.com/2005/08/03/technology/techspecial3/03randall.
html?pagewanted=2&ei=5070. [Accessed 14 March 2006].

Roberts, Gregory R., "Technology and Learning Expectations of the Net Generation,"
in *Educating the Net Generation*, ed. Diana G. Oblinger and James L. Oblinger
(Washington, DC: Educause, 2005), 3.1–3.17. Available online from   http://
www.educause.edu/TechnologyandLearningExpectationsoftheNetGeneration/6
056. [Accessed 5 December 2005].

The Secretary's Commission on Achieving Necessary Skills, U.S. Department of
Labor, "What Work Requires of Schools: A SCANS Report for America 2000"
(n.p.: U.S. Department of Labor, June 1991).

Smith, Kenneth R., "New Roles and Responsibilities for the University Library:
Advancing Student Learning through Outcomes Assessment" (paper prepared
for the Association of Research Libraries, May 4, 2000). Available online from
http://www.arl.org/stats/newmeas/outcomes/HEOSmith.html. [Accessed 10
January 2006].

Teaching and Educational Development Institute, *Pedagogy* (Brisbane: University of
Queensland, 2006). Available online from http://www.tedi.uq.edu.au/teaching/
toolbox/pedagogy.html. [Accessed 10 January 2006].

Western Association of Schools and Colleges, *WASC Handbook of Accreditation.
2001* (Alameda, CA: Western Association of Schools and Colleges, January
2001). Available online from http://education.berkelcy.edu/accreditation/pdf/
WASC_Handbook.pdf. [Accessed 5 December 2005].

Windham, Carie, "The Student's Perspective," in *Educating the Net Generation*, ed.
Diana G. Oblinger and James L. Oblinger (Washington, DC: Educause, 2005),
5.1–5.16. Available online from http://www.educause.edu/educatingthenetgen.

Engaging the Future: Meeting the Needs of NetGen

Jo Ann Carr

T he incoming generation of college students has grown up and gone to school in an environment substantially different from the one experienced by current college faculty and librarians during their years in elementary and secondary education. This chapter explores how these generational differences, resulting from changes in government oversight, societal expectations, authority structures, expected learning outcomes, course expectations, resources, and student participation, can contribute to a disengagement of students in higher education. The role of information literacy in bridging the gap between high school and college is demonstrated by numerous collaboration initiatives between K–12 and higher education.

Differences in K–12 and Higher Education

Ninety percent of today's high school freshmen indicate they plan to attend college[1] and 70 percent of high school seniors enroll in higher education within two years of graduating.[2] The general public sees a college degree "as the ticket of admission to a good job and a middle-class lifestyle."[3] Despite the aspirations of high school and college students and the expectations of society at large, major differences in K–12 and higher education contribute to a lack of engagement and thus lack of retention of students in higher education. When in college, 63 percent of students in two-year colleges and 40 percent of students in four-year institutions take some remedial education courses. About half of first-year students at community colleges and one quarter of students at four-year institutions do not return for a second year.[4] Most alarmingly, less than 20 percent of Latinos and blacks who begin community college go on to complete a bachelor's degree.[5]

As noted by David Conley in *College Knowledge,* the differences in K–12 and higher education stem in large part from the lack of a true system of education in the United States. In contrast to other countries in which the national government is involved in all levels of education, in the United States "two systems of education evolved in relative isolation from each other.[6] *The Governance Divide* further explores these differences by noting that "policies for each system of education are typically created in isolation from each other, even though, in contrast to the past, most students eventually move from one system to the others."[7] Although K–12 schools are part of a system within a district or perhaps within a state, there is no true "system" of higher education. Rather, higher education is highly differentiated by funding, institution type, age, demographics, mission, and prestige.

The attention of the public is focused more closely and critically on K–12 than on higher education because of the involvement of all levels of government as well as the number of students (53.8 million to 15.0 million), institutions (100,000 to 3,500), and teachers (3.5 million to 1.8 million).[8] This difference in focus also results in the identification of problems of success in higher education as the student's fault whereas lack of success in K–12 is attributed to problems in the system.[9]

The disconnect between K–12 and higher education also may stem from differences in the authority structure of these two institutions. "American high schools are, for the most part, rigidly authoritarian institutions that are so large that it's difficult for students to be known by name."[10] Attendance is taken, bells ring to indicate the end of class, and parents are often informed of problems in behavior and achievement. The nurturing atmosphere prevalent in elementary and middle schools has begun to give way to an atmosphere in which teachers may see themselves as life coaches, but not as nurturers in cognitive development.[11]

Although students may still not be known by name in their courses in colleges and universities, the rigid authoritarianism has given way to an enforced autonomy (and sometimes anonymity). This autonomy can lead to confusion and disengagement if students do not have the tools to connect with the myriad disciplines that are the basis of their introductory college courses. This different perspective on authority and autonomy also is reflected by students in higher education viewing themselves as consumers rather than as community members.[12] This new view of themselves is not surprising given the change in allegiance of the teaching staff from high school to college. High school teachers' loyalty is to their school, students, or profession whereas higher education's faculty's primary loyalty is to their discipline.[13] Unfortunately, neither authoritarianism nor autonomy fosters the student faculty interaction that is noted as one of five effective educational practices critical to student engagement.[14]

The gap in expectations regarding content to be learned was explored in *Understanding University Success: A Report from Standards for Success.* In this report, more than 400 faculty and staff from 20 research institutions responded to the query, What must students know and be able to do in order to succeed in entry-level university courses? In response, the contributors placed greater emphasis on habits of mind than on content knowledge. "However, the university faculty involved in creating these standards were most adamant in their assertion that success at research universities in particular is probably based more on mastery of the foundational skills than the content standards."[15] These foundational skills include problem solving, analytical and critical thinking, and communication skills.[16] All these skills are necessary for the active and collaborative learning that is another benchmark for effective educational practice.[17] Despite the information contained in the Standards for Success study, "students in K–12 rarely know what is expected of them when they enter college, nor do they have a clear sense of how to prepare for that next step."[18]

Differences in course expectations, in the use of textbooks, in assignments, in assigned resources, and in hours studying also contribute to differences in the engagement of students in K–12 and higher education. High school courses focus on memorizing content, interpreting information in a basic fashion, or simply completing assignments. Because science courses in high school focus on content, students in higher education "are unprepared for the conceptually oriented curriculum they encounter."[19] For example,

80 percent of college freshmen indicate that they are expected to engage in learning that requires analysis of the basic elements of an idea or theory rather than on a basic review of facts or data.[20]

In K–12 education, most students are assigned reading from textbooks designed to provide a structure for learning through the inclusion of advance organizers and review questions. In contrast, more than 49 percent of college freshmen were required to read more than eleven book-length assignments per year with as much as a book per week expected in courses in literature, history, and the humanities.[21] Critical reading and highlighting skills as an important aspect of information literacy are needed to bridge the "sometimes overwhelming shift from high school to college text books."[22]

The timing and frequency of assignments is another difference in K–12 and higher education. As noted in the "Guidelines for University Services for Undergraduates" in 2005, undergraduates are often enrolled in courses in which assignments have "short deadlines requiring timely library services."[23] Students must frequently complete assignments rapidly and independently of intermediate guidance from the faculty. In contrast, curriculum at the K–12 level is often structured in nine-week units in which students are guided through the assignment process with outlines, notes, bibliographies, and other components of assignments having specific due dates and separate grades.

Writing also is more intensive in college where expectations for writing papers of varying lengths and the need for writing something every week dominates.[24] Seventy percent of high school seniors wrote only three or fewer papers more than five pages in length. More than one-third of college freshmen write at least five papers five or more pages in length.[25] The assistance provided in identifying the resources in these writings also differs from high school to college. A survey by California State University Channel Islands indicated that high school faculty provide topics and resources to their students whereas college faculty expect students to identify information needs and locate the appropriate resources.[26] A discussion between high school and academic librarians in Wisconsin revealed a common practice in high school of encouraging students to use only resources in the local library, in stark contrast to the expectations of academic librarians in Wisconsin that students will use interlibrary loan and document delivery to locate the best resources on a topic.

The autonomy expected of higher education also extends to differences in group projects and class participation in high school and first-year college experiences. High school students report working on group projects 65.5 percent of the time whereas only 41 percent of college freshmen did so.[27] This difference may stem from the emphasis on introductory large lecture courses in the beginning classes in higher education. Unfortunately, recent emphases on achievement testing in K–12 may bring a closer correlation between K–12 and higher education as the testing environment parrots the same focus on parroting back content on multiple "guess" tests. In addition, this emphasis on drill and practice rather than on engaged learning results in a total disconnect between life and what is going on in the classroom.[28]

The difference in course expectations, learning materials, assignments, and the autonomy of learning contributes to a difference in the hours of studying for high school and college students. Whereas a third of seventeen-year-old high school students report studying at least an hour per day,[29] only 18 percent of college students spend as little as one to five hours on course preparation per week. The other students spent between 6 and 10 hours (24%), 11 and 16 hours (20%), 16 and 20 hours (16%), 21 and 25 hours (10%), 21 and 30 hours (6%), and more than thirty hours (5%).[30]

Differences in course expectations, use of textbooks, assignments, assigned resources, and hours studying may be a response to the different developmental stages of students in high school and in college. Much of the transferable learning that underlies the conceptual nature of college assignments is very abstract; these assignments pose particular challenges for adolescents who are not abstract thinkers.[31] The part of the brain, the prefrontal cortex, that is responsible for memory, planning, and organization is the last area of the brain to develop.[32] As a result, high school students may not have the capacity for independent conceptual learning until near the end of their K–12 careers or even after beginning their postsecondary careers. These developmental differences can also impact student engagement as students learn through "direct, concrete experience,...and a linear approach to learning" whereas faculty prefer global and abstract, and need a "high degree of autonomy in their learning."[33] Hersh further notes that "educators can assist students by identifying content that can be mastered by them semi-independently."[34]

Information Literacy and Student Engagement

The importance of information literacy is identified by Murray Sperber who, among his three cures for the "cancer" that afflicts undergraduate education, includes the abolition of large lecture courses and the promotion of interactive inquiry-based learning. Recognizing that large lecture courses owe their beginnings to the paucity of information sources, a far cry from the information glut of our current era, Sperber recommends that "students need to make sense of all the entries that bombard them during a database search."[35] The challenge of engaging students through information literacy is acknowledged by Doug Ackerman. After acknowledging that both Deborah Fallows's 2005 Pew study, *Search Engine Users,* and Stanley Wilder's January 2005 article in *Chronicle of Higher Education* cite the high confidence of high school seniors and college freshmen in their internet searching, Ackerman also notes that teenagers have a high degree of confidence in their driving ability, but "they're also the group that crashes the most often."[36] This misplaced confidence also applies to their use of technology, often creating a disconnect between what they already know and what they could learn to sharpen their skills and make their time online more effective, a disconnect that can be approached through information literacy and problem-based learning.

The connection between information literacy and the student engagement necessary to the successful transition between K–12 and higher education is defined in the 2005 NSSE report as deep learning. Deep learning is defined as the integration of reflective learning, integrative learning, and higher-order thinking that provides a more satisfying learning experience. One way to foster deep learning is to ask students to "identify and solve problems that require the use of multiple data sets."[37]

An examination of the *Information Literacy Competency Standards for Higher Education* demonstrates the correlation between information literacy and the "deep learning" needed for success in higher education. The abilities "to identify and access needed information, to evaluate sources, and to incorporate selected information into one's knowledge base" mirror NSSE's deep learning.[38]

This emphasis on deep learning supports the development of information literacy transition programs as high school instructional programs rarely "provide an intellectually coherent experience that cultivates the habits of mind."[39] Foundational skills in information literacy have been identified by the American Association of School Librarians as well as the Association of College and Research Libraries. An understanding of the role of these information literacy skills in deep learning in the content areas also is identified by David Conley who notes that "students need formal, progressively more complex experiences in researching. In a coherent program, students learn to formulate research questions, refine them, develop research plans, and find out what they already know about a topic."[40]

Conley also identifies the differences in information literacy skills for specific disciplines. In the social sciences, the "ability to find information from a variety of sources including the library and the Internet"[41] includes reliability, especially for online resources. An examination of the requirements for arts courses indicates that "Most arts courses at the college level require research skills in part because the creative process of producing one own's work usually raises questions about issues that are external to the piece."[42] The connection of information literacy to specific disciplines can contribute to the deep learning needed for student engagement by building up "layers of knowledge about how information is organized and accessed" and thus be "able to devise information research strategies.[43] However, connecting information literacy to specific disciplines requires that first-year students fully understand the concept of a "discipline." Therefore, information literacy for the disciplines must include an exploration of the context of the discipline and connection to its literature. As president of Brown University, Vartan Gregorian recognized the importance of information literacy in understanding disciplines of knowledge by quoting Richard Sheridan's *The Critic:* "The number of those who go through the fatigue of judging for themselves is very small indeed."[44]

Models for Addressing the Information Literacy Transition

First-year experience (FYE) programs, collaborative projects by state associations and institutes, and online resources are among the models for assisting in the information literacy transition. As noted by Scott Walter's bibliography for the First Year Experience Project, "it has only been in the last decade that truly collaborative efforts between FYE programs and academic librarians have resulted in the effective integration of higher-order information literacy skills into the FYE curriculum."[45] FYE programs foster a learning environment for new students to engage them intellectually, culturally, socially, and personally.

At California State Chico, the instruction coordinator was part of the faculty team for their first-year experience course. As part of the faculty, she was responsible for teaching a three-credit course as well as teaching her faculty colleagues in the areas of the information literacy curriculum which posed their greatest challenge: "the student e-mail program, the Internet, database searching, and the organization of information."[46] She also notes, "My better understanding of the students stems from having had extended opportunities to see what motivates and interests them and how they approach their assignments and learning,"[47] Another librarian noted his motivation: "I hoped to go beyond the limitations of the 'one-shot' bibliographic instruction session, enhance my interaction with students, and thereby become a more visible part of their community."[48] This approach also improved the FSP director's understanding of what librarians can contribute as participants in campuswide programs for students.[49] Information literacy can be effective in FYE programs as the data support the focus on first-year students as a group that responds to learning environments in which they establish, at a minimum, a comfort level for learning.[50]

Collaborations between K–12 and higher education are another way to support the information literacy transition. These programs help teach students "how to succeed within dysfunctional systems," a skill that is especially important for students who are first-generation college students.[51] One of the most structured of these collaborations is being funded by the Institute of Museum and Library Services and coordinated by the Network of Illinois Learning Resources in Community Colleges (NILRC). In this project articulation strategies and resources are being collaboratively developed by teaching staff and librarians at selected pairs of high schools and community colleges. Pre- and posttests on information literacy competencies of students at the beginning of their senior year through the end of their first year are being used to determine the effectiveness of these articulation strategies. Addressing the need to engage first-generation and underrepresented populations in higher education is a focus of this project, which includes the design and development of information literacy resources that address the unique needs of at-risk community college students.[52]

Another model of an articulated strategy for collaboration between K–12 and higher education is provided through the Institute for Library and Information Literacy Education. ILILE, also funded through the Institute of Library and Museum Services, sponsored a High School to College Transition summit in September 2004. Objectives of the summit focused on assisting students in increasing their confidence in their ability to succeed in college by lowering their anxiety about the transition; to orient students to the academic environment and culture; and to prepare students to do college-

and university-level research. The group noted the need to work with the Ohio Educational Media and Library Association as only one high school librarian participated in this summit.[53]

The New Jersey Library Association, the New Jersey Association of College and Research Libraries, Rutgers University, and the Educational Media Association of New Jersey collaborated in presenting a July 2004 program titled "Crossing Borders, Making Transitions: Information Literacy in Primary, Secondary, and Higher Education." This program reviewed information power standards from AASL, discussed strategies for collaboration, and identified the need to develop collaborative models in local communities.

Another example of a collaboration of regional cooperation is provided by the Community Libraries Outreach and Collaboration (CLOC), which is a voluntary group of school, public, and academic librarians in the Athens, Georgia, area. The initial activities of this group are to learn about the information literacy needs of students at all levels. In the long term, they plan to use this knowledge to develop a coherent information literacy program that stretches across curricula and grade level. CLOC also seeks to collaborate with other K–16 teaching initiatives in the northeast Georgia area to ensure that research skills are adequately addressed in the K–16 curriculum (CLOC). This emphasis on connecting information literacy to other aspects of the curriculum demonstrates a commitment to supporting student engagement by providing a supportive campus environment.

Additional examples of collaborative models between K–12 and higher education were identified by the AASL/ACRL Task Force on the Educational Role of Libraries. This effort was seen as "timely and appropriate" because of "the current focus on educational reform, the complex information technology environment, and emphasis on lifelong learning. Some new pedagogical strategies include standards-based education, outcomes-based education, inquiry learning, project-based learning, and service learning."[54] The importance of information literacy to student success in this new learning environment was stressed by the task force.

The development and use of electronic resources is a third model for promoting student engagement during the transition of students from K–12 to higher education. As stated by Ryan Ritz of Park Tudor School, "The key to teaching is keeping kids involved. They like everything electronic; it's speaking their language."[55] Another example of an electronic resource is the

University of Minnesota Libraries Assignment Calculator (http://www.lib. umn.edu/help/calculator/), which bridges the differences from the guided assignments at the high school level to the independence in work expected in higher education. The Assignment Calculator guides the undergraduate student through the process of developing complex assignments by identifying time lines for the steps in completing an assignment that are often graded as intermediate steps in high school assignments.

Other resources that speak "their language" include online tutorials to introduce college freshmen to the use of libraries and information resources in higher education. One example is CLUE (Computerized Library User Education) at the University of Wisconsin-Madison (http://clue.library.wisc. edu/). CLUE includes a module that discusses the difference between high school- and college-level research. This module introduces the concept of scholarly journal articles, the need to use sources beyond Google, and that new skills in locating these sources will be required. A second example is TILT (Texas Information Literacy Tutorial), which is designed to assist students "to explore and research in the online world" (http://tilt.lib.utsystem.edu/). TILT promotes active and collaborative learning by focusing on real-world issues and problems facing college students.

Recommendations for Fostering Student Engagement

The first and easiest step in fostering student engagement during the transition from K–12 to higher education is to talk with and develop cross-level teams with your counterparts at the K–12 or higher education level. The AASL/ ACRL standards or the *Knowledge and Skills for University Success* can serve as the basis of cross-level teams. Review of work samples and curriculum at the K–12 and higher education levels can foster a deeper understanding of the differences and similarities in the experiences and expectations of students in your local educational environment.[56] The importance of these local initiatives was identified in *The Governance Divide*, which notes that "state-specific contexts matter a great deal."[57]

High schools can participate in the Alignment and Challenge Audit from the University of Oregon, which provides high schools with information about how well their program of instruction aligns with postsecondary success standards. High school faculty then can adjust the content and challenge level of courses to better prepare students for college success. (See http://cepr. uoregon.edu/cepr.aca.php.)

The critical role that community and two-year colleges play in meeting the needs of first-generation and underrepresented students has been cited by both Conley and Hersh. The work of NILRC in meeting the needs of these learners can be replicated in other contexts and consortia to support the engagement of students in two-year colleges. The role of community colleges as an entry point for traditionally underrepresented students is critical to their ability to be admitted to and succeed at the four-year college level and beyond.

A key resource for assisting in the transition between K–12 and higher education is the Blueprint for Collaboration, which provides numerous recommendations for supporting student engagement by focusing on information literacy transition between K–12 and higher education. As a result of their work, AASL and ACRL have established a permanent Interdivisional Committee on Information Literacy, which is charged with sharing ideas on information literacy in K–20 environments. The Interdivisional Committee sponsors a listserv to foster discussions on the information literacy transition.[58]

Conclusion

A majority of today's high school students plan to attend an institution of higher education but are not prepared for the differences in authority structures, expected learning outcomes, course expectations, and learning resources that can affect their success in higher education. These differences can contribute to a lack of engagement if students do not have access to active and collaborative learning, faculty interaction, and a supportive learning environment. Well-articulated information literacy curricula and partnerships between K–12 and higher education can support student engagement by recognizing these differences and by designing programs, collaborations, and services that meet the needs of this new generation of students.

Notes

1. David Conley, *College Knowledge: What It Really Takes for Students to Succeed and What We Can Do to Get Them Ready* (San Francisco: Jossey-Bass, 2005), 4.

2. Andrea Venezia et al., *The Governance Divide: A Report on a Four State Study on Improving College Readiness and Success* (San Jose, CA: National Center for Public Policy and Higher Education, 2005), viii.

3. Richard Hersh, *Declining by Degrees: Higher Education at Risk* (New York: Palgrave Macmillan, 2005), 25.

4. Venezia. *The Governance Divide*, ix.

5. Hersh, *Declining by Degrees*, 189.

6. Conley, *College Knowledge*, 3.

7. Venezia, *The Governance Divide*, viii.

8. Hersh, *Declining by Degrees*, 12.

9. Ibid., 28.

10. Ibid., 233–34.

11. "Focus on the High School," *Mosaic* 7, no. 1: 4.

12. Hersh, *Declining by Degrees*, 28.

13. Ibid., 6.

14. National Survey of Student Engagement, *Exploring Different Dimensions of Student Engagement* (Bloomington, IN: Center for Postsecondary Research, 2005), 11.

15. Conley, *College Knowledge*, 169.

16. Ibid., 173.

17. National Survey of Student Engagement, *Converting Data into Action: Expanding the Boundaries of Institutional Improvement* (Bloomington, IN: Center for Postsecondary Research 2003), 11.

18. Venezia, *The Governance Divide*, viii.

19. Conley, *College Knowledge*, 75.

20. Ibid., 123.

21. Ibid., 121.

22. Amy L. Deunik, e-mail correspondence on Information Literacy Discussion List, Nov. 17, 2005.

23. "Guidelines for University Service for Undergraduate Students," *C&RL News* 66, no. 10 (Nov. 2005): 731.

24. Conley, *College Knowledge*, 122.

25. NSSE, *Exploring Different Dimensions of Student Engagement*, 30.

26. Amy Wallace, e-mail correspondence on Information Literacy Discussion List. Oct. 14, 2005.

27. NSSE, *Exploring Different Dimensions of Student Engagement*, 31.

28. Josh McHugh, "Syncing up with the iKid," *Edutopia* (Oct. 2005). Available online from http://www.edutopia.org/magazine/ed1article.php?id=Art_1355&issue=oct_05#.

29. Conley, *College Knowledge*, 121.

30. NSSE, *Converting Data into Action: Expanding the Boundaries of Institutional Improvement*, 33.

31. Camilla Baker, e-mail correspondence on Information Literacy Discussion List, Sept. 24, 2005.

32. "Focus on the High School," 3.

33. Hersh, *Declining by Degrees*, 160.

34. Conley, *College Knowledge*, 163.

35. Hersh, *Declining by Degrees*, 143.

36. Doug Ackerman, "Surviving Wikipedia Improving Student Search Habits through Information Literacy and Teacher Collaboration," *Knowledge Quest* 33, no. 5 (May–June 2005): 38.

37. NSSE, *Exploring Different Dimensions of Student Engagement*,17.

38. Information Literacy Competency Standards for Higher Education (Chicago: ALA, 2000), 3.

39. Conley, *College Knowledge*, 7.

40. Ibid., 81.

41. Ibid., 219.

42. Ibid., 236.

43. Topsy Smalley, "College Success, High School Librarians Make the Difference," *Journal of Academic Librarianship* 30, no. 3 (May 2004): 197.

44. Hersh, *Declining by Degrees*, 77.

45. Scott Walter, The First-year Experience and Academic Libraries:A Select, Annotated Bibliography (Sept 2004). Accessed at http://www.sc.edu/fye/resources/fyr/bibliography1.html.

46. Sarah Blakeslee, "Librarian in a Strange Land: Teaching a Freshman Orientation Course," *Reference Services Review* 26, no. 2 (1998): 74.

47. Ibid., 77.

48. Bruce Harley, "Freshman Information Literacy, Critical Thinking and Values," *Reference Services Review* 29, no. 4 (2001): 301.

49. Ibid., 305.

50. Sue Samson and Kim Granath, "Reading, Writing, and Research: Added Value to University First-year Experience Programs," *Reference Services Review* 32, no. 2 (2004): 153.

51. Venezia, *The Governance Divide*, 5–6.

52. Institute of Museum and Library Services grant, "Information Literacy for the 21st Century Learner:Preparing Students to Learn for Life." Accessed at http://www.nilrc.org/documents/IMLSfinalnarrative.doc.

53. High School to College Transition Summit. Accessed at http://www.ilile.org/ modules/initiatives/Past%20Events/index.php.

54. American Association of School Librarians/Association of College and Research Libraries Task Force on the Educational Role of Libraries. "Blueprint for Collaboration." Accessed at http://www.ala.org/Template.cfm?Section=school&tem plate=/ContentManagement/ContentDisplay.cfm&ContentID=59093.

55. McHugh, "Synching up with the iKid," 35.

56. Conley, College Knowledge, 77.

57. Venezia, *The Governance Divide*, 9.

58. To subscribe, send a blank e-mail message to subscribe-infolit@ala.org with your first and last name as the subject.

Bibliography

Ackerman, Doug, "Surviving Wikipedia Improving Student Search Habits through Information Literacy and Teacher Collaboration," *Knowledge Quest* 33, no. 5 (May–June 2005): 38-40.

American Association of School Librarians/Association of College and Research Libraries Task Force on the Educational Role of Libraries. "Blueprint for Collaboration." Available online from http://www.ala.org/Template. cfm?Section=school&template=/ContentManagement/ContentDisplay. cfm&ContentID=59093.

Baker, Camilla, e-mail correspondence on Information Literacy Discussion List, Sept. 24, 2005.

Blakeslee, Sarah, "Librarian in a Strange Land: Teaching a Freshman Orientation Course." *Reference Services Review* 26 (2) (1998) : 73–78.

Community Libraries Outreach and Collaboration. Available online from http:// www.libs.uga.edu/cloc/index.html.

Conley, David, *College Knowledge: What It Really Takes for Students to Succeed and What We Can Do to Get Them Ready* (San Francisco: Jossey-Bass, 2005).

Deunik, Amy L., e-mail correspondence on Information Literacy Discussion List, Nov. 17, 2005.

"Focus on high school" (2005) *Mosaic* 7(1) (2005pp. 2-5.

Gratch-Lindauer, Bonnie, "Information Literacy Student Behaviors: Potential Items for the National Survey of Student Engagement," *C&RL News* 66, no. 10 (Nov. 2005).

"Guidelines for University Library Services to Undergraduate Students," *C&RL News* 66 no. 10 (Nov. 2005): 730–37.

Harley, Bruce, Freshman Information Literacy, Critical Thinking and Values, *Reference Services Review* 29, no. 4 (2001): 301–306.

Hersh, Richard, *Declining by degrees: higher education at risk* (New York: Palgrave Macmillan, 2005).

_____, "What Does College Teach?" *Atlantic Monthly* 296, no. 4 (Nov. 2005): 140–43.

"High School to College Transition–Academic School Librarian Collaboration." Available online from http://www.ilile.org/modules/initiatives/Summit_09_04/Summit_09_04_Minutes.pdf.

McHugh, Josh, "Synching Up with the iKid," *Edutopia* (Oct. 2005). Available online from http://www.edutopia.org/magazine/ed1article.php?id=Art_1355& issue=oct_05#.

Macklin, Alexis Smith, "Integrating Information Literacy Using Problem-based Learning," *Reference Services Review* 29, no. 4 (2001): 306–14.

National Survey for Student Engagement, *Converting Data into Action: Expanding the Boundaries of Institutional Improvement* (Bloomington, IN: Center for Postsecondary Research, 2003).

National Survey for Student Engagement, *Exploring Different Dimensions of Student Engagement* (Bloomington, IN: Center for Postsecondary Research, 2005).

Roscella, Frances, "Crossing Borders, Making Transitions: Information Literacy in Primary, Secondary, and Higher Education," Presentation for Crossing Borders, Making Transitions Workshop, Brookdale Community College, NJ, June 9, 2004. Accessed at http://www.njla.org/njacrl/usered/events.html.

Samson, Sue, and Kim Granath, "Reading, Writing, and Research: Added Value to University First-year Experience Programs," *Reference Services Review* 32, no. 2 (2004): 149–56.

Smalley, Topsy, "College Success, High School Librarians Make the Difference," *Journal of Academic Librarianship* 30, no. 3 (May 2004): 193–98.

Tinto, Vincent, "Taking Retention Seriously: Rethinking the First Year of College," *NACADA Journal* 19, no. 2 (1999): 5–9.

Understanding University Success: A Report from Standards for Success (Eugene, OR: Center for Educational Policy Research 2003).

Venezia, Andrea, et al., *The Governance Divide: A Report on a Four-state Study on Improving College Readiness and Success* (San Jose, CA: National Center for Public Policy and Higher Education, 2005).

Wallace, Amy, e-mail correspondence on Information Literacy Discussion List, Oct. 14, 2005.

Walter, Scott, The First-year Experience and Academic Libraries: A Select, Annotated Bibliography (Sept. 2004). Available online from http://www.sc.edu/fye/resources/fyr/bibliography1.html.

Discovery Projects: Contextualized Research Experiences for College Sophomores[1]

Nancy S. Shapiro
Katherine McAdams

As in most action research,[2] the present study tells a story about teaching and learning. This story begins in 1996, when faculty and administrators at a large research university took a risk by attempting to involve sophomore students in the principles and processes of primary research. By introducing students to a method called Discovery, we introduced them to the world of university research with some remarkable results.

The Discovery method of teaching undergraduate research is based on three principles: First, the student, usually a sophomore, must choose a topic that is of great personal interest. Second, the student is coached by a mentor as he or she searches for relevant primary and secondary sources. Third, the student tells what he or she has learned through a poster presentation rather than a paper. By following the simple three principles of Discovery, hundreds of students have broken down barriers that keep research a world apart from bright students who, regardless of high scores and excellent grades, come to college thinking "What, me, a researcher?"

Since 1996, students at the University of Maryland have been literally getting into research through Discovery, taking pride in new abilities and in new status as researchers and presenters. This chapter explains the processes involved in using the Discovery method to introduce young college students to research and also tells the story of teachers and learners in the Discovery process over the past decade.

Why Sophomores?

The quality of undergraduate education at large research universities has come under considerable scrutiny and subsequent criticism over the past decade. Evidence from a variety of higher education assessment studies has clearly shown what many in higher education have suspected—that the undergraduates, far from benefiting from the rich resources of a research-intensive institution, are, in many cases, being shortchanged.[3] In 1998, with publication of the Boyer Commission Report on educating undergraduates in Research I universities, the issue rose to the top of the list of undergraduate reform initiatives. In an environment where the best teachers go unrewarded, where traditional large-class instruction limits active learning opportunities, and where enhancement moneys for research are funneled to faculty and their graduate students, rather than their undergraduate students, the Boyer report called for new models for undergraduate research.

Many universities have responded to these critiques by focusing on transforming the first-year experience, introducing interactive learning opportunities into large lecture classes, concentrating on teaching assistant training, and supporting improvements in undergraduate advising.[4] Popular programs that address undergraduate education beyond the first year include internships, experiential learning, service learning, and undergraduate research opportunities. However, many of these programs are targeted at junior- and senior-level students, leaving a vacuum in the second year, when undergraduate students are particularly vulnerable to academic "detours," yet developmentally ready to become intellectually engaged.[5]

Sophomore students are approaching an identity crossroads where they must, by the end of the year, declare a major, begin to seriously consider career directions, and confront decisions on a variety of developmental identity issues.[6] In addition, administrators are paying serious attention to persistence and retention after the first and second year of college. In his classic book, *What Matters in College?* Alexander Astin cites research that strongly suggests that strong faculty–student interaction "pays rich dividends in the affective and cognitive development of the undergraduate"[7] and impacts student success, satisfaction, and retention.

At its best, the second year can offer undergraduate students who have made a successful transition to college an opportunity to develop an appreciation of, or insight into, the ways in which research in their chosen field promotes changes in its fund of collective knowledge. At the University of Maryland, Discovery Projects was designed to draw students into the seductive mystery of inquiry, framing questions that have not yet been answered (or even asked) and seeking evidence that might lead to answers. The project described here introduces second-year students to the important stages of intellectual investigation, helping them develop strategies of independent inquiry and critical thinking while creating a logical transition where students can begin to see links between the academy, the society at large, and their eventual roles in that society. Their broadened perspective will help give them a context for the academic major- and career-related decisions they must make at the end of the second year. Discovery Projects grew out of an interest in finding new ways to stimulate student engagement in research while at the same time providing faculty with a framework for a structured undergraduate research process that would work across disciplines.

Role of Research for Undergraduates

Formalized research experiences are an effective means to promote student learning because the processes of inquiry and analysis tap into the potent combination of human drives to be curious about the unknown and to engage in the development of original ideas. Through their formative education years leading up to college-level studies, students are required to perform a variety of increasingly demanding assignments intended to expose them to certain aspects of the research process. Yet most, if not all, of those school-situated experiences are usually limited by the constraints of predetermined curricula and content objectives.

During the first two years at college, undergraduate research experiences also are constrained and limited by several realities. Because undergraduates, especially first- and second-year students, are not trained in sophisticated research methodologies, faculty frequently find themselves handing off undergraduate research projects to their teaching assistants. Even when a faculty member requires a research paper in an undergraduate course, the choices of topics and sources of information are generally prescribed to fit a certain course or topic (not dissimilar from students' high school experiences). Thus, students undertaking such projects typically view them as a "necessary evil" and, beyond the striving for a high grade, rarely invest much of their ego in the outcome. The third element that limits opportunities for learning in project-oriented research is the palpable absence of a larger audience beyond the instructor.

The idea of promoting research-based experiences for college undergraduates, particularly those at research universities, is not new. University-sponsored research internships, with undergraduate work on projects directly tied to faculty research programs, are perhaps the most widely used vehicle for exposing students to the research environment. They have the advantages of using existing faculty resources and afford students rewarding views of knowledge creation at "the cutting edge." In exceptional cases, students may develop an extended involvement with a project; they may be included as coauthor on a publication or be inspired to pursue a related career path.

In practice, however, it has been the experience of faculty at many universities that there are several problems with this scenario. Even if faculty were inclined to work with undergraduates, the entry barriers are high. The inexperience of the undergraduate students, their relatively short-term availability for extended projects, and their crowded schedules of course work, workplace obligations, and activities all act as barriers to involvement in serious research on faculty-initiated projects. In fact, Astin's study goes so far as to suggest that faculty research priorities can sometimes negatively impact undergraduates.[8]

Of the few remaining opportunities for faculty-guided undergraduate research, juniors and seniors have a decided advantage over those who are still engaged in foundation course work and are less familiar with the university culture.

Developing a Better Model: "Owning the Question"
Discovery Projects creates new opportunities for undergraduate research that connect second-year students with sites outside the university by creating a kind of research internship. By providing a simple, structured method for involving undergraduates in research, Discover Projects bridges the gap between freshman writing assignments and upper-division capstone research projects in their majors.

The purpose of Discovery Projects is to contextualize particular knowledge and situate it in the real world. The projects have three elements: First, they define limited, but engaging, tasks of uncovering/discovering primary source materials. Second, they provide an authentic purpose and audience for novice researchers by linking them to carefully selected sites outside the university, such as schools and other nonprofit information-gathering groups and institutions. Finally, the Discovery Project model creates research frameworks in the form of procedural guidelines and small research cohort groups that provide technical support for participating faculty mentors by establishing a "self-guided" instruction kit for independent research.

The Discovery Project model was designed to be developmentally appropriate, grounding student research experiences in concrete, primary resources such as printed documents, photographs, tapes, diagrams, maps, and other artifacts. Discovery Projects emphasizes student learning of the processes of research, rather than a final paper. Development of the model was based on a pilot study that took place in 1995 at the University of Maryland College Park Scholars Program, a residential living–learning community supported jointly by academic affairs and student affairs offices.[9] In that pilot project, twenty students in a Science, Technology, and Society thematic learning community were invited to work alongside professional historians, archivists, and display artists with materials in the Smithsonian Institution's Lemelson Center for the Study of Invention (in Washington, DC). They were invited to contribute to the mission of the Lemelson Center by creating instructional Invention Discovery Kits for use by public schools and educational groups. Over the course of the semester, each student identified a mentor and worked independently to assemble primary documents and artifacts on inventions of his or her choice, interviewed the inventors or members of their families or friends, and prepared hands-on learning packets (literally, a box full of reproduced documents, sketches, photographs, and tapes) for the Smithsonian to archive and use as educational materials for outreach to elementary and secondary schools. Two examples illustrate the concept:

> Shannon, a sophomore business major, decided to investigate the "straightening comb," invented by Madam Walker, one of the most remarkable African American women entrepreneurs at the turn of the century. According to Shannon, the investigation took her from the U. S. Patent Office to documents associated

with Madam Walker and the Harlem Renaissance. Shannon collected copies of original patent documents and interviewed one of Madam Walker's surviving relatives—her great-great granddaughter. She gave these raw materials to a public school for elementary and middle school students to use as part of their Black History Month projects.

Elliot, a sophomore with a strong interest in music, opted to investigate the origins of the electric guitar. He worked with historians and archivists, tracking down leads and documenting his "discovery path" in ways that led the Smithsonian archivists to decide to develop an exhibit on the electric guitar over the next several years. Elliot was invited to participate in the planning of the exhibit.

Of particular importance in these examples is the notion that if students are investigating something that has already engaged their curiosity, they are much more likely to "own the question" and experience the excitement of discovery. Professor Charles Striffler (University of Maryland), mentor to the two students above, noted that students who engaged in the Discovery Projects developed "an enthusiasm for learning." Almost the entire original pilot group of students pursued their project far beyond the one-credit commitment that had been built into the original design, and the single biggest complaint was that both students and faculty felt that one semester was not nearly enough time. A number of students asked to continue their work through independent research credits into the next semester. In his final written report, Dr. Robert Shoenberg, evaluator for the project, commented, "Faculty were particularly pleased that a large number of students formed an effective mutual support group and listserv on their own and that many of the students had gotten 'bitten by the research bug.'" [10]

The innovative Discovery Projects model also was influenced by its home in College Park Scholars (CPS), a growing and successful living–learning community for freshmen and sophomores. (See www.scholars.umd.edu.) In CPS, all sophomores are expected to engage in an active learning project, usually in the form of service learning, independent research, or internship.

Discovery Projects: A Brief Description

The original project developed as a successful proposal to FIPSE (Fund for the Improvement of Postsecondary Education) and targeted four objectives:

Objective 1: Students will join in an introduction to research course that will teach steps and stages to the research experience; they will learn research skills and pursue independent research projects.

Objective 2: Students will reflect on their own research and on the process of research; by engaging with primary sources, they will develop confidence in their own ability as researchers.

Objective 3: Discovery Project students will experience improvement in overall student academic success, satisfaction, and retention.

Objective 4: Discovery Project students will benefit from increased contact with faculty, staff, and other subject matter experts.

Initially, the Discovery Project model for undergraduate research was developed and field-tested (and later adopted on campus) as a course, CPSP259, Discovery Project Research in College Park Scholars. Following is the typical set of Discovery Projects workshops that would be included in any syllabus for CPSP259:

Week 1: Introduction to Research
Week 2: Placing Your Research in Context: Secondary Sources
Week 3: Research Questions, Scope, Methods
Week 4: More on Methods
Week 5: The Processes of Research
Week 6: Presenting What You Have Learned: Preparing for the Academic Showcase

Initially, instructors were librarians who had special expertise in working with undergraduates. Later, the course was taught by advanced Ph.D. students who had been trained in teaching undergraduate research. These instructors, known as Discovery coordinators, conducted the workshops and helped students learn basic research techniques; however, students were instructed to select a faculty member or other mentor to provide advice on specific content and sources for their projects.

While in the Discovery Projects course, student researchers form a community of peer learners who gathered to discuss their research, learn undergraduate research skills, and reflect on the nature of knowledge. Each student kept a log book, reflecting on process and progress. Students collected and prepared their findings for an academic audience assembled at the conclusion of the course, usually in the form of an Academic Showcase with poster presentations.

Discovery Projects offered multiple opportunities for one-on-one interactions between students and mentors and with selected subject matter experts. The overall focus of the Discovery Projects curriculum is on the processes of discovery rather than products, so these projects culminate in poster presentations at a Campus Undergraduate Research Fair rather than in research papers. The research fair required that students prepare a poster-board presentation, with an annotated "log book" that explained their starts and stops and their process for overcoming inevitable hurdles and blind alleys.

The model for Discovery Project research may be summarized best by the following "Steps in a Discovery Project," a class handout given to students when they are introduced to Discovery Project work that prescribes the following steps:[11]

1. The student will develop and confirm a research proposal with the Discovery Coordinator. This proposal will be briefly summarized in the Discovery Projects logbook in the section titled "Statement of Purpose."

2. The student will begin gathering secondary research materials on the selected topic. We suggest a minimum of five secondary sources to put your topic in context.

3. The student will further narrow the major research question and begin collecting primary research materials. This may involve trips to the National Archives II, Greenbelt Museum, Holocaust Museum, or to sites around the Washington, D.C., area to interview scientists, inventors, journalists, or other sources.

4. Once immersed in primary and secondary materials, the student will further narrow the question and scope of the project to be sure that the work can be completed before the Academic Showcase.

5. The student will keep a record of primary and secondary source information in his or her Discovery Projects logbook.

6. The student will record observations and reflections on sources, interviews, documents, conclusions, and workshops in the logbook.

7. The student will attend all five Discovery Projects workshops and write evaluations of the workshops in the logbook.

8. The student will meet at least twice each semester with his or her faculty director, either via e-mail, in person, or by phone, to let the director know how the research is progressing and what is being learned. Students use this opportunity to ask questions or let the Coordinator know of problems.

9. The student begins to analyze the collected information and to make decisions about what they have found and what they need to find. As if writing a story, the student pieces together the primary and secondary resources to formulate answers to research questions.

10. Each student will consider what is most important or interesting about what they have found and address the question of why the findings are of significant interest to others. The student will record the significance of the research project in the Significance Statement in the logbook.

11. Each student will attend the workshop on presentation, then put together a collection of what was found and learned and organize a poster display. Students may include materials such as tape recordings, original documents, pictures, secondary resources, plant samples, or whatever may be appropriate to describe what has been discovered.

12. Students will present their poster displays at the Academic Showcase to an audience of peers, professors, parents, and community members.

13. The student will complete the writing prompt and all evaluations that are included in the logbook, then hand in the completed logbook to the appropriate instructor or faculty member (for example, a student in Life Sciences would be hand in her logbook to the director of CPS Life Sciences).

14. Each student can celebrate the success of having completed a Discovery Project!

Discovery as journey

The Discovery Project often is described as a journey. In a letter to prospective Discovery Projects students, CPS faculty explain the metaphor:

> Think of your Discovery Project as a trip through a foreign country. Your passport into the project is your research idea, described in your research proposal. This describes where you want to go and what you want to see.
>
> You have several guides to help you on your trip: Your faculty director, the Discovery Projects coordinator who is your teacher, archivists and many others who have knowledge of your topic and materials related to it.
>
> As you travel, you will carry a suitcase with you—your logbook. This is where you will keep reflections from each site you visit, describe what you are learning, and write about connections you see. There will be two main ways of learning about the country you are visiting. First, you can learn by actually being there and visiting the museums, monuments, documents, and famous sites (primary sources); and, second, by reading the history, background, or interesting facts about these artifacts to place them in context (secondary sources).
>
> Along the way, your guides will host several gatherings or "workshops" as we call them, where you will sit down with your fellow student travelers and talk about a particular part of your trip, what to expect next, how to make sense of what you are learning, and what has been different for each of you. At the end of the semester, you will consider how you can gather all the different experiences into some form that can be presented to your teachers, family, and community so they can have a glimpse of what you have learned. When you decide how to present your experiences, you will gather with your guides, fellow travelers, family, friends, and community for our Academic Showcase, where you will tell a story of how and what you discovered.[12]

Creating a Campus Culture for Undergraduate Research: A Culture of Evidence

Initially, it was not easy to persuade faculty to use Discovery Projects as a capstone experiences in their College Park Scholars courses. Several professors voiced doubts about the appropriateness of primary research for lower-division students; others worried about the time commitment involved in mentoring undergraduate researchers. Eventually, however, the faculty themselves became strong advocates of the project, in part, because evidence of success was collected to document the evaluation of the federally funded FIPSE project. The project results described below demonstrate types of evidence that were collected during the FIPSE project that have been used to justify a substantial institutional investment undergraduate research.

Logbooks

Students used their logbooks in unanticipated ways that revealed much about the subprocesses of research. It was expected that students would treat logbook entries as formal writing; instead, students used these entries as personal, reflective spaces where they discussed the struggles, frustrations, and (sometimes) delights of research. The project evaluator, Robert Shoenberg, noted the "cathartic" nature of the logbook entries. Logbooks provided a place for students to reflect on their own Discovery processes and report what they learned from the difficulties they faced. Students cited a desire to go beyond just collecting facts. They revealed a strong interest in "raising the bar for themselves" by making sense out of what they found and telling the story. The evaluator noted that students "craved" the opportunity to present, when they felt they had a story to tell. And the story, rather than the collection of facts, seemed to be what they were after. In their logbook entries, students repeatedly cited particular trouble with narrowing topics and with efficiently accessing and making sense of primary materials. These repeated themes, along with the desire to "raise the bar" and tell the story, led project administrators to develop workshops focused on these research tasks. At the same time, it also was decided that the logbooks and what students wrote in them were of research interest in and of themselves and could be used as an evaluation tool.

Interviews

Robert Shoenberg conducted half-hour interviews with twenty-two students and twelve faculty members over the course of three years. Throughout these interviews, he found widespread expression of pride, satisfaction, struggle, and even joy in the remarks of the students when they talked about their Discovery Projects. He writes, "No one regrets doing a Discovery Project." He described the uniformly positive reaction students had to the experience and the "strong emotional response" they had to the primary source materials. The contents of student logbooks repeatedly echo this journey from frustration to satisfaction.[13]

Interviews with students indicate that during their course work, or even one to two years afterward, students have a limited view of what the experience has given them. When asked by the evaluator about the long-term benefits of Discovery Projects participation, students most often cited their close working relationships with faculty, some of which resulted in teaching or research assistantships in the junior and senior years. Others mentioned good preparation for working alone on an intense project. However, students uniformly said they saw no connection between their Discovery Projects and career formation, although anecdotal evidence suggests that some connection does exist. Six former scholars have become McNair Scholars, where they begin a transition to graduate study. Many others have completed honors theses in their majors.

Improved Writing and Research Skills.

FIPSE funding for the Discovery Projects initiative required that independent researchers and consultants be called in for objective assessment of student learning over the three years of the grant. After the first year, a team of faculty in the areas of freshman writing and professional writing conducted a series of studies to examine the progress of the twenty-nine students who were Discovery pioneers. Using rubrics to examine pre-and postessays about research, the research team found that 77 percent of students showed improved competence in their writing skills.[14] Using the same technique, they also found that 73 percent of Discovery students showed improved skills for finding information and 61 percent showed an improved writing process. Based on these findings, along with their analysis of extensive interviews with the students, Colson and Callahan concluded:

> Many students seem to gain expertise from doing the research
> projects (that is, they learn some lessons about research), which

in turn makes them more competent researchers. Students…are more likely to see the distinction between primary and secondary sources. Students are likely to see that research has some distinct stages, even if they cannot articulate all the stages. Students are also more likely to evaluate sources for bias and reliability as a result of their Discovery Project experience."[15]

Similar findings emerged in assessment interviews conducted by Robert Shoenberg, noted earlier, and also in a separate assessment of a 2001 group of summer Discovery students. Since 1999, the Discovery method has been used to help rising juniors and seniors develop research projects for the Ronald E. McNair Scholars program.[16] As an assessment activity for the McNair program, instructors in the research course gave students a pre- and postsurvey that included seven questions concerning comfort with the practice of research. Analysis of the pre- and postsurvey responses showed that, for the 2001 McNair group, comfort increased for all aspects of research except for research presentation. The summer Discovery students reported improved comfort with many aspects of research, including work with primary and secondary sources and with the research process.

Retention/Diversity Statistics

Although it would be inappropriate to attribute increased retention to a single factor, such as participation in the Discovery Projects, a study of students who completed the projects indicates that those students were retained at a higher rate than others in the selective College Park Scholars program. Although more research needs to be done to tease out causal relationships and correlations, the external evaluator felt confident in claiming that student participation in the undergraduate research experience seems to correlate positively to greater retention/persistence and graduation.[17] Sophisticated analysis of both the retention statistics and the interviews led the evaluator to conclude that Discovery Projects did have an influence that is distinct and separate from other positive forces in the College Park Scholars living–learning program.

One final note is warranted on diversity and Discovery. Minority students made up 25 percent of Discovery Projects population over the four years of the grant, and some faculty mentors suggested that the Discovery Projects may appeal to students of color because they encourage students to investigate difference as an academic topic (i.e., projects such as Firestone in Nigeria and Japanese Internment: Racist Intentions). Many such projects were produced by students of color, and others who felt underrepresented in traditional undergraduate course content. It is clear that in addition to learning about basic research, students used Discovery Projects as a way to explore differences and expose injustices. Data analyzed by the program evaluator indicate that these minority students, in their junior and senior years, were more likely to be retained than non-Discovery Projects students in any minority group. Success with McNair and with diverse students in Scholars suggests that further research is needed on the appeal of Discovery Projects to nontraditional students.

Student Voices

Ultimately, the students themselves best express their experience with Discovery projects. Following are some examples of responses to the final prompt in the Discovery logbook:

> I used to shudder when I heard the word *research*. However, the more experience that I encountered with this topic, the more comfortable I have become with it.

> Before this archives project, my idea of research was the study of compilation of other people's compilations...never before had I confronted the real thing—the original document, the memo, the press release, the confidential case file—and been forced to draw the interpretations and make the connections on my own. It was an amazing rush having to figure things out for yourself like this.

> After completing this Discovery Project, I am able to address research on a much more advanced, sophisticated level...I have used many tools throughout my research process that are beneficial for all researchers.

These student reactions demonstrate a level of competence and confidence that regularly appeared as by-products of reflection on the work of Discovery Projects. One student expressed a new comfort in the presence of researchers:

I also learned to work well with my advisors, my research mentors, librarians, and archivists. This is a big change considering that I was very intimidated by all of these people before I began this research project.[18]

In the students' voices we hear a theme repeated in interviews and in logbooks: the undergraduate experience was enhanced by the interaction with program faculty and staff. The student comments also serve as a reminder that Discovery Projects occur early in the college students' cognitive developmental pathway. These are very young students, and it should come as no surprise that they still have difficulty seeing themselves in authentic roles as researchers and academics. Their increasing comfort in the world of research may be for many a first step toward graduate school or to a scientific or medical profession.

At the beginning of the project, no one expected Discovery Project students to care about their research as much as they did in most cases as shown in logbook entries and through evaluation forms and exit interviews. The 200 College Park Scholars who participated literally heaped praise on the Discovery program. After each Discovery workshop (and there were six each spring), students filled out a qualitative/open-ended evaluation form. In virtually all the evaluations, students voiced praise for some aspect of Discovery Projects, such as the following:

I liked that we were "forced" to do research today.

I liked that we are guided in our work and that we also have the freedom to work individually.

I am starting to think that I am interested in sociological studies.

I have the potential to make this project really good, as long as I utilize my time and resources.

I realized I can research.

Amid the praise in their logbook entries, students agreed that there were three major difficulties with Discovery Projects. First, more than half the students mentioned that they had trouble and needed help narrowing their topics for research. Many of these students went on to say that after the topic was narrowed, the research proceeded smoothly. One student summed up the sentiments of many others, saying,

> The most difficult part of my research was narrowing down my topic and then getting started. My topic was broad, and there were many different avenues that I could've taken, so that it was very difficult for me to pick out the most interesting point.

Another student commented that "getting started" was the hardest part, but that "once that is done, and you start to get into the flow of things, it is almost as if you are carried along by the information you are discovering, which makes you want to find all the information you can and tell the best possible story."

Time management was another challenge for students. Students wished for better time management skills and berated themselves for failing to budget time spent between readings and seeking primary sources. Most concluded, however, that completing a Discovery Project had helped to make them better students because they gained a realistic understanding of this universal limitation on research—time must be managed, and that skill must be mastered.

Finally, students cited the problem of finding relevant materials. In many cases, this problem reflected their difficulties in finding appropriate topics or research questions. Students also said they found libraries and archives "intimidating" but agreed that faculty and staff quickly solved their problems when they were asked. Keeping lines of communication flowing between students and information specialists is of critical importance to the successful completion of the projects.

Many students hinted in their workshop evaluations at needing more guidance and help. When these workshop evaluations were processed, the next few classes were devoted to one-on-one help sessions. Students also voiced resentment about "forced" trips to the library or computer lab, saying they could have accomplished more on their own computers in their rooms. An equally common theme in the evaluations, however, was gratitude for a "forced" trip to the library or lab.

Final whole-course evaluations, which are part of the logbook, also were glowingly positive. Here are some typical final comments:

I learned just how many resources are out there. I didn't realize there were so many.

I learned about UM and its students, and how to develop a research project. Though I have done this in other classes, this class allowed me to see what others were doing and other methods of completing the project.

I *experienced* way better than a class or a lecture. I carry with me an extensive understanding of the workings of a criminal investigation, DNA profiling, hair and fiber analysis, and how popular culture has influenced crime itself!

I learned to look and end up in a topic that was not my first intent. Going from one question to another. Learning research management.

Themes such as these came up repeatedly: immense satisfaction in exploring an area of personal interest, sharing with other students, seeing that one question may have many answers, and appreciating the rich variety of sources available on even the most obscure topics.

Faculty Experiences

Like the students, faculty consistently gave positive evaluations to Discovery Projects. The FIPSE outside evaluator interviewed all faculty at the end of each year; in addition, a graduate assistant interviewed all Discovery faculty at the conclusion of the grant in 2000. Both found consistent satisfaction among faculty. The outside evaluator found that faculty were "pleased" with their students' Discovery experiences and "appreciated" the richness that Discovery Projects added to their curriculum without imposing an excessive burden. Discovery was seen as an especially suitable project in Scholars because it involved active and interdisciplinary learning, which are hallmarks of College Park Scholars.

Over the four years, faculty also wished for more focus on the research product than was originally intended. They liked the emphasis on the Discovery process but found that students floundered without more direction on how to produce a good poster or presentation. In the end, Discovery Projects required students to balance their emphasis on process and product, while faculty had to balance their desire for quality products with the messiness of the intent of true "discovery."

At the conclusion of the grant, faculty told our graduate assistant for assessment that they liked the esprit de corps that developed among groups of students as they worked on Discovery and also the displays of "enthusiasm and confidence" by students who completed Discovery Projects. The also said they witnessed "imagination and creation" in their students.

Faculty responded in uniform ways to questions about problems they had with Discovery. All agreed that some uniform treatment of credit awarded for Discovery would be a good idea. At the same time, they liked using their own specialized approaches to Discovery, adding such extra requirements as conference presentations, panels, and papers, that resulted in different credits earned. Faculty members were so committed to these innovations that they repeatedly resisted changes that would result in a uniform awarding of credits across programs.

Faculty also voiced concerns over knowing when to leave students alone with their struggles and when to step in and help. These questions about the correct level of supervision persisted over the four years of the grant. Faculty looked to Discovery staff, to their instructor's notebooks, and to each other for guidance on when and how to intervene with a student's research process without exerting too much influence. Some faculty said they were not sure sophomores had a good understanding of "what truly interests them" and that even topic selection processes needed close supervision. The outside evaluator commented that, overall, more faculty supervision was needed for Discovery than was originally envisioned when the grant was proposed. (In these phases of the project librarians might possibly play a more central role than originally envisioned, and Discovery staff could offer workshops to help faculty better manage student needs and demands. Such workshops could appropriately frame work with Discovery students as professional development activity).

Over time, faculty members were willing to try Discovery Projects again and again despite the challenges. Sometimes they tried innovations (team projects, for example, or special themes such as the Civil Rights movement or the Cold War) and almost always approached the next year by fine-tuning and improving the logbook, the course syllabus, and the pattern of contact with students. Faculty also commented that the 1998 instructor's manual was a helpful innovation.

Dr. Albert Gardner, professor in the College of Education and faculty director for Scholars in the Advocates for Children program, lifted the Discovery Project pilot to a broader campus level. As a member of the Lilly Fellows (an honorary group faculty associated with excellence in teaching), Dr. Gardner proposed that the campus place more emphasis on undergraduate research. Based on his success with Discovery Projects, he persuaded his group of Lilly fellows to organize the first campuswide Undergraduate Research Day on the University of Maryland Campus on April 26, 2000. Many kinds of undergraduate research projects were presented on that day, including nearly 100 Discovery Projects. Since 2000, the university has continued the tradition of celebrating an annual spring Undergraduate Research Day. Recently, the College Park Scholars program announced an endowed prize for outstanding undergraduate research.[19]

Summary and Conclusions

In addition to the evaluation evidence of the positive impact on students, an unexpected and equally positive impact was felt by participating faculty and staff. Project staff summarized the learnings from the project in the following analysis:

Top Ten Lessons Learned about Undergraduate Research[20]

1. Faculty–student contact is not as important as mentor–student contact. The point is to design a meaningful relationship between the student and someone who has studied and is very knowledgeable about the student's research area. This person may or may not be a faculty member at the university.

2. Undergraduate students need a strong, consistent, peer-support group while they are doing undergraduate research. This group should meet regularly and reflect together with a faculty/staff member on the challenges they are facing and celebrate the breakthroughs.

3. We cannot overestimate the importance of students choosing their own topics. When students choose research topics for personal reasons, or from their own intellectual curiosity, they are intrinsically motivated for independent learning, and what they discover is that much more important to them.

4. When first- and second-year students engage in undergraduate research, especially a Discovery Project using primary source materials, there is

a shift in their understanding of the nature of knowledge and truth. Students no longer see knowledge as something outside of them, and begin to see it as something they can create.

5. The research process for beginners is, and should be, a struggle. Students should be given a good balance of challenge and support, but we need to feel comfortable letting students struggle with defining their questions, narrowing their scope, and analyzing their data.

6. Beginning researchers need a well-defined point of entry. They need research methodologies that they can cut their teeth on. Some kinds of interviewing, document analysis, basic surveying, and a lot of historical research lend themselves nicely to this concept.

7. It is important to build as much structure as possible into independent research projects for undergraduates. Learning contracts, progress reports, mandatory meetings, and mid-semester annotated bibliographies are key to keeping students on track. These activities also provide them with time on task.

8. The best experiences define the scope of the undergraduate research project early on, and do not leave students wondering what is expected of them.

9. Students who spend time each week reflecting upon the progress of their research, next steps, and what they are personally learning about the process, in a journal or logbook, have better projects and take away more value from the experience.

10. Students need to be able to present their discoveries to an audience of peers, faculty members, parents, and mentors. They gain important communication and professional skills by preparing to present their research findings at an academic showcase. But most of all, presentation is an important capstone, bringing closure to the entire experience.

Discovery projects work because the sum of their parts is simply good teaching. In his book of lists, "What the Best College Teachers Do," Ken Bain points to many best practices that are also Discovery basics:

Knowledge is constructed, not received.
Start with the Students Rather than the Discipline.
Create a Natural Critical Learning Environment.
Help the Students Learn Outside of Class.
Create Diverse Learning Experiences.[21]

Bain reminds college teachers that "caring is crucial" and "questions are critical," also guidelines for Discovery projects, and he reminds all who teach that "Human beings are curious animals. People learn naturally while trying to solve problems that concern them."[22] This basic understanding of human nature is at the heart of every Discovery project.

A Final Word

The Discovery Project model places "discovery" at the center of students' learning experiences in college. Discovery Projects is anchored by faculty mentors, peer groups, and the necessary discipline of deadlines, logbooks, and public presentations. The importance of "owning the question," which is a critical part of all authentic research and the essence of the Discovery Project model, can best be appreciated by allowing the students to have the last word:

> I think what I learned in this project was different from other classes because my research and learning was entirely interest driven. I got to dictate the direction of my own learning.

> I learned that research doesn't have to be boring and tedious. It taught me to look at research in a different light, something that can be fun and interesting.

> Aside from what you can put in a paper, research is so much more. There is not always one answer. This project has infiltrated every aspect of my life (something that can't be said about most of my other classes).

Notes

1. Discovery Projects was supported by a grant from the U.S. Department of Education. FIPSE Grant number P116B61181. Nancy S. Shapiro PI and project director 1996–1998; Katherine C. McAdams was project director in 1998–2000.

2. John Elliott, "Evidence-based Practice, Action Research and the Professional Development of Teachers," Goldsmiths Journal of Education 2, no.1 (1995): 1–15.

3. Association of American Colleges, Integrity in the Curriculum: A Report to the Academic Community (Washington, DC: Association of American Colleges, 1985); Study Group on the Conditions of Excellence in Higher Education, Involvement in Learning: Realizing the Potential of Higher Education (Washington, DC: National Institute of Education, 1984); Wingspread Group in Higher Education,

An American Imperative: Higher Expectations for Higher Education (Racine, WI: Johnson Foundation, 1993).

4. M.L. Upcraft, John Gardner, and Associates, The Freshman-year Experience (San Francisco: Jossey-Bass, 1989); Alexander Astin, What Matters in College? Four Critical Years Revisited (San Francisco: Jossey-Bass, 1993); George Kuh, "Guiding Principles for Creating Seamless Learning Environments for Undergraduates," Journal of College Student Development 37, no. 2 (1996): 135–48.

5. William G. Perry, Forms of Intellectual and Ethical Development in the College Years: A scheme (Austin, TX: Holt, Rinehart and Winston, 1970).

6. Ibid.

7. Astin, What Matters in College? 342.

8. Ibid., 338.

9. Nancy S. Shapiro and Jodi H. Levine, Creating Learning Communities: A Practical Guide to Winning Support, Organizing for Change, and Implementing Programs (San Francisco: Jossey-Bass, 1999).

10. Final evaluation report, submitted to FIPSE, May 31, 2000, 9.

11. Final evaluation report, submitted to FIPSE, May 31, 2000, 11.

12. Final evaluation report, submitted to FIPSE, May 31, 2000, 11–12.

13. Final evaluation report, submitted to FIPSE, May 31, 2000, p. 14.

14. Beth Callahan and Mike Colson, "Report on College Park Scholars Discovery Projects: Comparison of Student Pre- and Post-essays" (unpublished paper, University of Maryland, College Park: May 5, 1998).

15. Ibid., 13.

16. The McNair Scholars program, sponsored by the U.S. Office of Education, supports minority students who plan to pursue doctoral studies. Students come to selected campuses for summer research and mentoring. The university has been a McNair campus since 1990, and first-year McNair students have used the Discovery method to develop their research projects since 1998.

17. Final evaluation report, submitted to FIPSE, May 31, 2000, 14.

18. Final evaluation report, submitted to FIPSE, May 31, 2000, 15.

19. Nancy and Ira Shapiro Excellence in Undergraduate Research Award, established 2005.

20. From a handout prepared for dissemination materials by CPS Discovery project staff.

21. Ken Bain, What the Best College Teachers Do (Cambridge, MA: Harvard University Press, 2004).

22. Ibid., 46.

Bibliography

Association of American Colleges, *Integrity in the Curriculum: A Report to the Academic Community* (Washington, DC: Association of American Colleges, 1985).

Astin, Alexander, *What Matters in College? Four Critical Years Revisited* (San Francisco: Jossey-Bass, 1993).

Bain, Ken, *What the Best College Teachers Do* (Cambridge, MA: Harvard University Press, 2004).

Boyer Commission on Educating Undergraduates in the Research University, *Reinventing Undergraduate Education: A Blueprint for America's Research Universities* (Washington, DC: Carnegie Foundation for the Advancement of Teaching, 1998).

Callahan, Beth, and Mike Colson, "Report on College Park Scholars Discovery Projects: Comparison of Student Pre- and Post-Essays" (unpublished paper, University of Maryland, College Park: May 5, 1998).

Elliott, John, "Evidence-based Practice, Action Research and the Professional Development of Teachers," *Goldsmiths Journal of Education* 2, no.1 (1995): 1–15.

Kuh, George, "Guiding Principles for Creating Seamless Learning Environments for Undergraduates," *Journal of College Student Development* 37, no. 2 (1996): 135–48.

Perry, William G., *Forms of Intellectual and Ethical Development in the College Years: A scheme* (Austin, TX: Holt, Rinehart and Winston, 1970).

Shapiro, Nancy S., and Jodi H. Levine, *Creating Learning Communities: A Practical Guide to Winning Support, Organizing for Change, and Implementing Programs* (San Francisco: Jossey-Bass, 1999).

Study Group on the Conditions of Excellence in Higher Education, *Involvement in Learning: Realizing the Potential of Higher Education* (Washington, DC: National Institute of Education, 1984).

Upcraft, M.L., John Gardner, and Associates, *The Freshman-year Experience* (San Francisco: Jossey-Bass, 1989).

Wingspread Group in Higher Education, *An American Imperative: Higher Expectations for Higher Education* (Racine, WI: Johnson Foundation, 1993).

Personally Engaged Information Literacy in General Education through Information Ecology and Fieldwork

Darren Cambridge

There is an emerging consensus that information literacy is an important component of general education, and there is widespread agreement that enhancing student engagement is an important goal. How, then, should we teach information literacy in an engaged way in general education courses? In this chapter, I examine my redesign of the course NCLC 249, which I teach in New Century College at George Mason University, in light of these issues. From my experience, the way NCLC 249 has traditionally been taught exemplifies some limitations of narrow conceptions of what students need to know about information. The course's limitations help illustrate that a full embrace of engagement requires a more situated approach. I offer my response to these limitations by redesigning the course to illustrate the process by which these broader ideas about an engaged process to information literacy can be put into action.

NCLC 249: The Internet is 200-level course that introduces students to understand and use the Internet critically and effectively. It is offered within New Century College, an integrative studies program with a competency-based curriculum that emphasizes interdisciplinarity, learning communities, and experiential learning. Although some students take the course as part of a New Century College concentration and others as part of a minor in multimedia, most members of the class use it to fulfill general information technology requirements. It draws students from a variety of programs and academic years. Originally designed by Virginia Montecino in fall 1999, it now is offered each semester and taught by a variety of instructors. Course activities are designed to help students use the Internet to find, evaluate, synthesize, and communicate information; to communicate and collaborate using a variety of media; to design documents for online publication; and to think critically and reflectively about information and information technology. The course includes a service learning component through which students work with nonprofit organizations on projects that utilize their knowledge of the Internet. I first taught it in the spring of 2005. My analysis here is based on that experience, discussions with other instructors, past and present, and a close review of past syllabi, Web sites, and other course materials. Prior to my involvement, NCLC 249 was a highly valuable course and considerable evidence points to its effectiveness in enhancing students' information literacy. The rather lengthy critical appraisal that follows is intended to suggest how to build on its strengths, not to belittle its already significant accomplishments.

From Student to Personal Engagement

Implicit in the design of NCLC 249 is a commitment to an engaged approach to information and information technology. To see how engagement enriches information literacy in a general education context, I need to say what I mean by the term engagement. The term can be thought about in three different ways. The first two are most prominent in the literature. First, "student engagement" is defined at the amount of "time and energy students devote to educationally purposeful activities," activities that have been shown to correlate with deep learning and other desired outcomes.[1] Thus, everything from completion of active learning assignments in the classroom to active participation in certain types of cocurricular activities counts as evidence of engagement on the part of students. This definition underlies the popular National Survey of Student Engagement.

Since its inception, NCLC 249 has been designed to encourage student engagement. The design of course activities, both within and beyond the classroom, has been informed by research on promoting deep learning and effective use of technology. Students read, discuss, critique, and extend the ideas of leading thinkers about information and technology. They are active learners, receive rapid feedback, engage in substantive revision, and find authentic audiences for their work. Classes are taught seminar style, in networked classrooms, and feature intensive discussion and exploration. Students take responsibility for their own learning and are given considerable opportunity to be self-directed. This focus on deep learning is common to all New Century College courses and may explain NCC's exceptionally high NSSE scores. The DEEP project identifies NCC and George Mason University as a model for encouraging student engagement.[2]

The second perspective on engagement is what is usually called public engagement. This is often encountered in the literature on the role of the public university in society, which argues that universities must become more genuinely engaged with the communities in which they are located, moving beyond service toward a genuine, two-way exchange of knowledge that serves the needs of both the community and the institution over time.[3] This version of engagement is also operative in the scholarship of engagement movement, which seeks to redefine work in the community and the application of knowledge across disciplinary boundaries to socially important problems as scholarly work that should be recognized as an integral component of faculty careers.[4] There is a long tradition of engaging students in public engagement through service learning and other pedagogies for the public good.[5]

NCLC 249 is part of this tradition. Service learning has been a component since its inception. Each semester, students locate a partner with whom they work with the assistance of the Center for Service and Leadership, which initiates and maintains relationships with a wide variety of community organizations throughout northern Virginia and the Washington, DC, metropolitan region. In collaboration with their organization, students develop objectives for a 45-hour project that both enhances their learning in relationship to the goals of NCLC 249 and advances the organization's work. Students have taken on such challenges as building Web pages for community arts councils, teaching recent immigrants how to communicate online in public libraries, crafting Internet-based public education strategies for environmental research groups, and researching public health resources for Pacific Islanders.

I'd like to suggest a third type of engagement, which I'll call personal engagement. In this way of thinking, people are engaged when the practice of inquiry saturates their life. People are engaged to the extent that they embrace the full complexity of the human experience and use the habits of mind they develop, in part, through formal education to grapple with that complexity across all the spheres of their lives. Students are personally engaged when they use the knowledge, skills, attitudes, and abilities they have learned in the classroom, and beyond it, in their personal, professional, and civic lives. Personal engagement also is in evidence when what's learned in those contexts shows its face in the classroom. Personally engaged students fuse their engagement in educational activities (student engagement) with their engagement with their communities (public engagement) and their engagement with other parts of their lives that fall outside these domains. These students no longer police the boundaries. People are personally engaged when they examine the total of their lives-as-experienced and act on the basis of what they learn.

Engagement here is close to integrity, in the sense of both integrating multiple types of knowledge, experiences, identities, and communities and cultivating a consistency of commitments over time. As does public engagement, personal engagement has a moral dimension. It is about deciding to be a reflective person who lives the human experience with eyes wide open. In the words of the IUPUI English Department's mission statement, it is about making a commitment to living "the examined life: a thoughtful, morally aware, and civically and personally responsible existence."[6]

Doing so means moving beyond the set of lenses, problems, and communities that are the focus of a particular academic discipline and grappling with the complexity of life-as-experienced in a seemingly untamable range of contexts. It requires acknowledging the values of multiple communities and finding a way to forge identity that both coheres with the values and practices of the group and remains consistent across them. It requires grappling with our embodied experience and the materiality and contractedness of human experience. It requires understanding how who we are, what we care about, what we choose to do, and the ideas, environments, and tools that mediate these activities are deeply intertwined. An engaged approach does not try to abstract away this complexity. Rather, it embraces it and tries to articulate it in order to inform how we should act.

From Conventional to Personally Engaged Information Literacy

NCLC 249, as I first taught it and as it had traditionally been taught, did a far less effective job of cultivating personal engagement as it did public and student engagement. Although demonstrating an uncommon commitment to community service and deep learning, the course still reflected a limited understanding of information literacy and technology. These limitations may be shared by many general education courses that intend to help students become more literate with information and fluent with technology. I'd like to unpack the limitations of the conventional view, as exemplified by NCLC 249, by contrasting a narrow interpretation of the Information Literacy Competency Standards for Higher Education with a broader reading that moves us toward personally engaged information literacy.[7] The following section explains how this broader reading informed the redesigned version of NCLC 249.

Even from a brief acquaintance, it is clear that a commitment to student engagement is at the core of the information literacy movement. Indeed, many of the skills central to the prevailing conceptions of information literacy also are essential to the full range of pedagogies that researchers are finding effective in promoting deep learning. The standards argue that information literacy is important to students "in their academic studies, in the workplace, and in their personal lives." It "forms the basis for lifelong learning," which is "central to the mission of higher education institutions." This focus on lifelong learning in a variety of contexts suggests that information literacy is necessary for effective public engagement and that it may be able to serve as a bridge between different spheres of activity for the personally engaged. Rigorous inquiry requires information literacy, and a commitment to inquiry throughout life is central to personal engagement. The justification of the value and conceptual scope of information literacy in the standards is consistent with valuing public and personal engagement. However, the more granular outcomes specified in the standards can be interpreted in a manner that marginalizes this dedication. Although this narrow reading likely does not reflect the intentions of the standards' authors, it may often be found in practice, such as in the traditional way of teaching NCLC 249.

From Abstract Skills to Situated Expertise

The standards can be read as defining information literacy as a set of skills that are independent of the context in which they are needed. For example, an information-literate student "describes criteria used to make information decisions and choices." A designer of a general education course might find in this statement an assumption that decisions about how to find and use information should be guided by a set of criteria independent of any particular context, any particular group of people and set of material circumstances.

NCLC 249, as it was traditionally conducted, focused on such relatively context-free skills for evaluating information. For example, in my spring 2004 version, students produced annotated bibliographies on some topic related to the Internet that they posted on their own Web sites. Through their selections and annotations, students demonstrated their facility in summarizing and evaluating information using general principles such as authority, objectivity, timeliness, and accuracy.[8] The judgments were framed as universally valid and made public online for a potentially broad, but largely undefined, audience. This was certainly a valuable activity, helping students learn the conventions of the sort of academic literature review they were likely to need to perform in future academic research projects.

Beyond the classroom, however, decisions must be made in accordance with the dynamics of local practices, values, and constraints within specific communities of practice. Communities of practice are informal groups in which members share common problems and objectives and learn from each other over time.[9] For example, Julian E. Orr investigated the failure of an expert system designed to help Xerox copy repair technicians.[10] By what we might think of as globally valid criteria for making information decisions, the system should have been a stunning success. The database provided a mechanism for collecting detailed information about what works, made it easy to organize that information logically, and made the information widely accessible to technicians acting independently in the field. In addition, it provided powerful search tools. However, Orr's ethnographic research into how technicians actually solved problems in the field showed that the traditional practice of communication within the community of practice of technicians, one-on-one through two-way radios, proved considerably more effective. Although seemingly inefficient and prone to error, the process of sharing stories about past repair experiences and collaboratively talking through issues helped experienced technicians share tacit knowledge, knowledge not yet made codified, that they would not have thought to record in the official system in response to specific contingencies of the problem currently at hand. Reasoning together with their more experienced colleagues, novices learned not just facts about what can go wrong with a particular model and when, but also how expert members of their profession reasoned through complex problems. Understanding the need for information within the context of the larger work activity and the network of relationships between actors in multiple roles within the informal structure of the community was here more important than global principles for systematic acquisition and evaluation of information.

General education courses need to move beyond just teaching decontextualized skills to also help students understand and act effectively within these authentic social and technical networks. Service learning projects provide an opportunity to observe and participate in using information in such rich contexts. However, to take advantage of this opportunity, the information literacy curriculum must include a broader set of methods. As discussed below, the fieldwork methodology provides a powerful compliment to traditional humanities-style research.

From Disciplinary Differences to Contextualized Values

A limited reading of the standards also could lead an instructional designer to attribute differences in the way information is created, organized, and used solely to differences between academic disciplines at a global scale. For example, an information-literate student "differentiates between primary and secondary sources, recognizing how their use and importance vary with each discipline." Presumably, this means that students understand, say, that psychologists prefer to make judgments based on experimental data whereas philosophers often rely more on their interpretations and extensions of the writings of other philosophers. For understanding and participating in scholarly discourse, this makes good sense. In workplace settings, however, the preference for primary over secondary sources may have no clear link to any disciplinary community. Even within settings where disciplinary values clearly come into play, such as a community organization that conducts environmental research, a host of local factors influences how information is valued and used that may be as important as the global, disciplinary commitments to understanding how to use information well within this local community of practice. Within such an organization, even for those trained as biologists or chemists, public perceptions about environmental threats and priorities may hold considerably more importance than they would in a university research lab.

NCLC 249 is offered by New Century College, an integrative studies program staffed by faculty members from across the disciplinary spectrum. Many courses take a postdisciplinary approach, combining methods and methodologies from many academic traditions to particular challenges and objects of study.[11] The integration of the best of what a range of disciplines can offer in response to the contingencies of a particular context, be it academic, personal, or organizational, is a core value of the college. NCLC 249 has traditionally attempted to bridge disciplines, combining instruction in research, information technology, and communication, using texts that range for pragmatic expositions of technical operations to highly theoretical accounts of philosophical and social issues. However, even within this environment, NCLC 249's approach to information literacy has been constrained by differences in disciplinary-based approaches to research. Although not tied to a single discipline, the literature-based focus of most of the research assignments featured in most offerings of NCLC 249 clearly reflect what Hugh Burkhardt and Alan H. Schoenfeld call the humanities approach.[12] They argue that research methodologies can be grouped into three categories, categories that are often also used to group academic disciplines.

The humanities approach centers on the examination, synthesis, and extension of a collection of what has been written or said about a topic. (This chapter largely takes this approach.) The science approach focuses on the systematic, direct observation of phenomena. The engineering approach involves creating, testing, and refining processes or tools. Although students may participate in online communities or discuss their experiences using information in organizations and daily life in class, direct observation has generally been subordinated to writing from sources. Students may observe information practices in the field through their service learning, but they are not generally asked to gather and analyze those observations systematically. Although the instruction students receive in developing online texts may engage the engineering tradition, students usually have had few opportunities to test their designs in authentic contexts. A truly integrative approach would balance and connect all three perspectives.

The service learning component of the course offers numerous opportunities for observation, analysis, and intervention. However, it has traditionally been loosely coupled with the rest of the course. Although students may be asked to give presentations about their projects and may bring them up in class discussions, rarely have they been encouraged to apply the methods of inquiry they learn in class to understanding how to work effectively in their partner organizations. Conversely, they have been unable to reintegrate the insights gained from their work in the field in a formal way with their classroom-based work on understanding the role of information and technology in society.

Although the primacy of disciplinary epistemologies and identities may hold within traditional academic settings, it is much less powerful in the broader contexts in which students find themselves using information in their communities, workplaces, and personal lives. Important distinctions about what counts as information and what information is most valuable often do not align with disciplinary differences.

For example, David Weinberger offers an example of searching for information online about a new washing machine.[13] Although he found technical details on the manufacturer's Web site (buried beneath layers of empty marketing material) and he has easy access to the analyses of professional reviewers in periodicals, his decision is swayed much more strongly by discussion group postings. These postings have are biased, incomplete, and idiosyncratic. They feel like the authentic voices of real people who speak from the vantage point of someone who has experienced how the machine fits into everyday life. One writer notes that the buzzer that rings when a load is complete is extremely loud. As Weinberger notes, it's unlikely that any salesperson would have pitched "check out the buzzer on this baby," that such a detail would have made it into a traditional review or, if washing machines were deemed an appropriate object of study in some field, an academic research project. In this case, Weinberger values an understanding of the role of the machine within the rhythms of the daily life of his household. Whether or not it wakes the baby may prove to be more important than how many towels it can wash in a load. Because even a home is a complex system of people, activities, and technologies, a systematic, neutral observer alone may not even know the right questions to ask without the experience of integrating the machine into such a system.

Weinberger's investigation of washing machines is made in a personally engaged way and clearly demonstrates a kind of information literacy. Making use, in part, of the research process he's learned in higher education, he's determining what he needs to know, seeking out a variety of types of information, and evaluating the results and using them to guide an important experience in his personal life. The way he judges the authority of the information he locates, however, differs from that employed in academic research processes we often teach—as decontextualized or disciplinary skills— in general education courses. It might be possible to talk about the different values and sources of authority here in terms of disciplinary epistemologies, but it makes more sense to shift focus to asking students to experience and reflect on a variety of such complex environments and to participate in the use of information, utilizing multiple methods, within them in order to build their information literacy through authentic action.

In this example, the technological environment of the Internet makes it possible to gain access to the embodied knowledge that Weinberger values for its reflection of the complexity of lived experience rapidly and over great distances. In this new environment, he argues in Small Pieces Loosely Joined, authentic written voices, positioned within the threads of conversations, have a new power that balances traditional sources of institutional and scholarly authority.[14] Those established strong voices through consistent contributions to Web conversations become "authorities without qualification."[15] The experience of using the Web show that "professionalism is a role and politesse is an artifice" designed to hide imperfection and suppress dialog.[16] Authenticity comes from the author's demonstration of his or her "situatedness" through expressions of passion, biases, limitations, which manifest themselves in decisions about "tone of voice," "style of paragraph," or choice of links.[17] How these choices about textual techniques are made are shaped by the conventions of the community through which conversation occurs, and knowledge of those conventions is another sign of credibility.

Authority also comes from the ability to maintain interest, to capture detail, and to convey narrative structure. In both online and local organizational settings, scholars are increasingly seeing the value of narrative in guiding decision making and building relationships.[18] Indeed, narrative itself is being revealed as an important tool in the process of inquiry. According to Weinberger,

> making a decision means deciding which ... "inputs" to value and how to fit them together to make a coherent story. In fact, the story helps determine which of the inputs to trust by providing a context in which the inputs make sense.[19]

This circular movement between source of information and narrative context helps uncover what is intriguing and what is surprising. It helps direct our attention toward what we did not know we needed to know. Weinberger suggests that knowledge on the Web can be sorted into two categories: the database and the joke. "Databases let you look up information. ... jokes ... reveal what you weren't expecting. ... Laughter is the sound of sudden knowledge. ... Jokes are all about context."[20]

In teaching information literacy in general education courses, we do a much better job teaching the database than we do teaching the joke. We need to do a better job of helping students to recognize and communicate their passions and to reflect on how what they care about impacts how they find and evaluate information. We need to help them understand the complexity of the contexts in which information is shared and used, contexts not reducible to disciplines or courses. Students need to become better able to cultivate a strong voice in which other members of the conversations they join find authenticity, better able to craft narratives that capture the details of their local contexts and the drama of sudden realizations using the conventions of new contexts and drawing on the power of new relationships.

Rather than a single disciplinary context, fully engaged students will encounter multiple, overlapping communities of practices as they exercise their information literacy throughout their civic, professional, and personal lives. Every community has its own values about information and knowledge, its own way of distributing the processes of information use, constraints of the material and technological environment, and preferred media, modes, and genres of communication. In addition to the multiplicity of communities, students are faced with a social environment in which conventions of communication are quickly changing, and a diverse set of tools are available and in use. Students need to understand and rapidly adapt to changes in this complex network of elements and relationships in order to understand how to find, evaluate, and synthesize information effectively within these social contexts. Effective information literacy will mean finding a place within the network.

From Individual Skills to Distributed Activities
In contrast, a narrow reading of the Information Literacy Competency Standards could frame information literacy almost exclusively as an individual skill. Although it may be important to understand disciplinary practices and larger "economic, legal and social" contexts, most of the process of using information is performed individually by the student. He or she may consult with instructors and librarians along the way and will need to communicate the end product of the research process to some audience, but the bulk of

the work is done solo. The research activity is clearly the traditional academic research project within the humanities or, perhaps secondarily, scientific traditions.

In contrast, in the organizational settings in which students are likely to use information beyond the classroom, individual actions are often part of a larger activity that involves multiple people and a variety of tools. The activity involves a complex coordination of actors, human and technological. As Ed Hutchins demonstrates in *Cognition in the Wild*, the thinking in these activities can often not be fully understood as a collection of individuals acting autonomously.[21] Rather, understanding how information is used in the larger activity requires an understanding of distributed cognition, framing the searching, evaluating, and synthesizing are a collective product of the system of people and tools. For example, Hutchins shows how the navigation of a Navy vessel depends on complex interactions of crew taking measurements with optics, calculating, contextualizing and error checking with maps, communicating and aligning coordinates through information systems, interpreting and making course corrections, sending the right directions to the right place, and putting those directions into action through sailors in multiple roles operating steering and propulsion systems in coordination. The work of gathering information, analyzing it, making decisions, and acting on them is not the product of individual thinking, nor is it reducible to what goes in inside the human mind without reference to the material, technological environment. Understanding how to use information effectively in this high-stakes activity requires looking at the whole system of people, practices, and tools.

Most iterations of NCLC 249 have included a collaborative research project. From working together to investigate an Internet-related topic, students have gained valuable experience in group interaction. However, these projects have generally been indistinct from individual research projects except to the extent that they are performed by multiple people. Work is generally divided up to minimize dependencies, and students are largely left to their own ingenuity in determining how to coordinate their work. Groups are rarely informed by a history of collaborative practice. Service learning projects have generally been even more solitary, performed by individual students applying individual research and technology skills, largely without explicit attention to the place of the discrete project within the larger processes of using information and technology within the community organization.

Rather than mastering individual research techniques, effective use of information in collaborative activity requires understanding how activity is distributed throughout distributed systems such as those Hutchins describes. Armed with this understanding, students can determine the optimal relationship of their individual actions to the whole. Further, they are equipped to identify opportunities of change and improvement in tools, practices, and roles throughout the system.

From Disinterested Information to Embodied Technology

From this systems vantage point, technology is not simply a means to an end, to be engaged or not as individuals choose, but an integral part of a distributed activity that shapes and is shaped by other elements of that system. If information literacy is to be extended to embrace this understanding of socially contextualized, trans- or antidisciplinary, integrally collaborative and distributed information use, its teaching cannot be disengaged from teaching about technology. The standards contend that information literacy is a broader than fluency with information technology because with the latter,

> the focus is still on the technology itself. Information literacy, on the other hand, is an intellectual framework for understanding, finding, evaluating, and using information—activities which may be accomplished in part by fluency with information technology, in part by sound investigative methods, but most important, through critical discernment and reasoning. Information literacy initiates, sustains, and extends lifelong learning through abilities which may use technologies but are ultimately independent of them.[22]

Implicit in this statement is the idea that information has an essence distinct from its material instantiation in the tools used to record, process, and communicate it. There are a set of intellectual skills for dealing with information in its essential form, and these skills are distinct from those required to understand the tools we regrettably have to use to interact with it. Technology often gets in the way of our access to this pure, unmediated information, and so learning how to use and understanding it is a necessary evil. In the ideal world, no such mediation is necessary, and the goal of information technology development should be to minimize the impact of the materiality of tools in the practice of using information. Paul Duguid called this ideology "liberation technology."[23]

A systems view, however, sees technology as an integral component of human activity whose development and use complexly intersects with information structures, practices, and relationships. David M. Levy recounts the history of the contemporaneous rise of rationalized control and impersonal management, emergence of the memo, and development of the typewriter and carbon paper, and vertical files at the beginning of the twentieth century.[24] The new management style required more systematic and extensive record keeping and intra-organizational communication, resulting in formation of the new genre of the circular letter or memo. Memos were initially circulated person to person according to a distribution list, but the typewriter and carbon paper made it possible to provide separate copies to each individual employee and gave management the ability to make it more difficult for them to determine who else had the information and restricted their ability to annotate it as it made its rounds. However, the vertical file made it possible for individuals and branches to maintain records of these communications, distributing the institutional memory and providing new opportunities for holding centralized management accountable. According to Levy,

> although the memo emerged as a tool of the new management techniques, it also shaped them ... the new management methods and the new document technologies and genres co-evolved, with changes in one affecting the others.[25]

In order to become information-literate participants in the workplace, students must be able to navigate these coevolutionary processes. In addition to learning to work within distributed systems of information activity that include people, tools, and ways of working, students must understand how these systems change in order to begin to imagine how they can be improved. However, understanding change at the scale that Levy describes does not yet equip students to affect change within their spheres of influence in the authentic networks in which I have argued an understanding of information literacy must be rooted. Students also must understand change at the local level through engagement with communities of practice beyond the classroom as they function and evolve.

Through such activities as building Web pages, manipulating images, and using scholarly databases, NCLC 249 has traditionally performed well in acquainting students with fundamental skills necessary for using common information technologies. Through reading and writing about social theory and contemporary issues as they manifest themselves in the media, NCLC 249 also has invited them to think about how technology impacts society. Through the service learning project, students are exposed to authentic local contexts in the community in which people, technology, and the practices distributed across them coevolve. However, these activities have not been tightly interested. The classroom focus has been primarily on either research within an academic context or broad cultural–historical patterns of change and global discussions of issues such as gender, access, and privacy. NCLC 249 has not taken full advantage of the engaged, authentic context of the service learning site to apply both technical skills and attention to social and technical relationships and change processes to the dynamics of the local, situated use of information. Students have generally also not been asked to extend the broad analyses of technology, information and values they encounter in the readings to the choices they make about the roles of technology and information within their lives, both within and beyond the campus community.

Shifting the focus to local systems where change is possible and toward choices about information and technology throughout the many spheres of students' lives requires students to examine their own positionality, to chart their relationships to people, practices, and tools in a variety of social contexts in order to see how their assumptions influence how they navigate those relationships and make sense of what they learn. As Weinberger argued, articulating such relationships and how they influence one's decisions is often central to persuasive participation in communities, particularly online, that value the traces of embodied experience in conversation.

Understanding and communicating one's position is central to understanding technology as system. It means shifting attention to the experience of information, not just its essence.[26] Levy, for example, examines several editions, print and digital, of Whitman's *Leaves of Grass* in relationship to his own experience of the text over time and his affection for the edition he owned as a child to show how the meaning of the text is shaped by changes in the textual content, choice of illustrations, affordances of the book and the browser, and the role of a particular artifact in his own biography. Judging the value of the poem requires understanding each of these aspects and their relationships from Whitman's identity, experience, and choices. He argues that a fuller understanding of information and its "enabling technologies" may require us to recognize "how form, content, and medium are not-to-be-fully-separated constituents in our lives and in the richness of our experiences."[27]

From Neutrality and Resistance to Critical Engagement

Bonnie A. Nardi and Vicki O'Day suggest that the dominant metaphors used in writing about technology depersonalize it, either casting technology as value neutral or as part of a global system we as individuals are powerless to change.[28] Technology is often about writing as a tool with a set of technical features that have no necessary relationship to social practices or values. To use it effectively, one need simply choose the right tool for the job. Thinking about technology as tool obscures the role of the larger contexts in which it is embedded, its complex history of coevolution in relationship to people and practices within communities.

In contrast, many critical theorists treat technology as a system that has far-reaching consequences for the structure of social life. This line of thinking is epitomized by Jacques Ellul's concept of *technique*, "a cultural mindset in which pure, unadulterated efficiency is the dominant cultural value."[29] Technique, woven into both technical systems and institutional structures, becomes an autonomous force independent of human value that does not adapt to the needs of people, but to which people must adapt. It pervades all realms of human activity. The immense scope and reach of technology as a system provides little opportunity for individual agency. Our only viable option is to resist technological society. However, a personally engaged approach to information technology requires identifying opportunities to shape the role of technology in the use of information, not a wholesale rejection. We must find ways to be "critical friends of technology."[30]

The impact of both these metaphors in NCLC 249 is clear. Much of the teaching of technology skills in the course has traditionally focused on a set of software tools, helping students learn what capabilities each has and what sorts of tasks each can be used to complete. However, this instruction was largely divorced from consideration of the contexts in which the tools were developed and their relationships to the network of people, practices, and values students might encounter in those contexts in which the tools might be deployed. Many of the readings, in contrast, considered technology as a largely autonomous system, favoring critical distance over critical engagement. Even those readings that focused on the positive aspects of technology trended toward the "rhetoric of inevitability," treating technological change and the accompanying changes in social practices as forces beyond of the control people's activity in everyday life and independent of local values.

From this analysis, it's clear that transforming NCLC 249 into a course that centers on personally engaged information would require significant reorientation, changes that would likely be needed in many general education courses that focus on information literacy. Greater emphasis would need to be placed on analyzing and acting in authentic communities of practice, online and in the physical space, articulating the complex relationships within distributed systems of people, practices, and tools working with information. Students would need to understand how these systems change over time. They would need to discover the values operating within those systems, reflect on how they relate to their own, and develop a voice that shares that understanding in order to shape that change.

Metaphor, Methods, and Integration

This transformation would require a shift in the metaphors used to frame inquiry, a shift in methods taught for conducting that inquiry, and a more integrative approach to course activities. In the fall 2005 semester, I taught such a transformed version of NCLC 249 for the first time. The new version centers on the idea of the information ecology in order to shift focus to local, distributed, changing networks of information activity. It emphasizes fieldwork as a methodology that compliments traditional humanities research. Through reflective and field writing, it places students' experience and engagement in community organizations and across multiple spheres of life at the center of classroom activity.

Information Ecologies

Understanding the multiple, complex contexts in which students use information as information ecologies is now a primary goal of NCLC 249. Nardi and O'Day "define an information ecology to be a system of people, practices, values, and technologies in a particular local environment."[31] Like the critical theorists whose work has traditionally been a part of the curriculum, the conceptual framework of the information ecology treats the use of information as a complex system of human activity. However, it shifts focus to the specificity of local environments. The scope of an information ecology is bounded by the capacity of people who are part of the system to change it. "Local is now defined by influence in an ecology—which comes from participation and engagement—and commitment to a set of shared motivations and values."[32] Effective participation in an information ecology requires engaging in a process of inquiry into relationships among the people, practices, values, and tools that use information within that local scope and engaging others in dialog about the results. In a well-functioning information ecology, people are regularly engaged in a process of strategic questioning that examines how "social values and policies, as well as tools and activities" fit together.[33]

Although quite compatible with the idea of a community of practice, a concept I've used throughout this piece, framing these local systems as "information ecologies" rather than communities has several advantages. Both focus on systems of collaborative activity mediated by a matrix of tools, conventions, and techniques, but the ecology metaphor emphasizes the need for ongoing transformation and stresses the inherent value of diversity more strongly than does community.[34] Coevolution is a key feature of information ecologies. Information ecologies use information within a larger context of rapid social and technological change. In healthy information ecologies, "people's activities and tools adjust and are adjusted in relation to each other, always attempting and never quite achieving a perfect fit," cultivating "a balance found in motion, not stillness."[35] The ability to coevolve in the face of change is facilitated by diversity, another key facet of information ecology. The presence of "different kinds of people and different kinds of tools" working together provides a wider of range of possible responses to the challenges the system may face in use information over time.[36]

A truly engaged information literacy, put into action beyond the classroom, should equip students to advance the collaborative process of investigation that characterizes well-functioning information ecologies, tracking the dynamics of coevolution and discovering the resources of diversity in how information, technology, and identity intersect. Moreover, it should help them begin to see patterns across the multiple, authentic ecologies in which they participate in their academic, civic, personal, and professional lives. Although such participation requires the traditional humanities-style academic research skills often taught in general education courses such as NCLC 249, a much broader skill set is necessary to investigate the information practices and tools not neatly abstracted and classified within the structure of scholarly knowledge. Students must be equipped to investigate the dynamics of information use within their information ecologies and learn to argue for the conclusions they draw in relationship to what these systems value.

Fieldwork

Fieldwork is a methodology well suited for investigating and creating dialog within information ecologies. Like information ecology, fieldwork emphasizes how the values, norms, rituals, behaviors, and artifacts that are part of the activities of a group add up to a coherent whole and how they have evolved throughout the history of that group. Like information ecology, fieldwork focuses on the local, postponing generalizations and global judgments in favor of deep understanding of a particular set of social and material relationships, situated within a particular context.

Although it can include research using the scholarly literature, fieldwork includes a variety of methods—such as interviews, structured direct observation, analysis of artifacts, and reflective writing—that enable fieldworkers to engage with a much broader range of sources of information better suited to entering the complexity of systems of information use in the wild. Fieldworkers triangulate between multiple types of evidence to develop a systemic understanding of the cultures they investigate and participate in. They strive to balance the voices of their informants, the participants in cultural system, the voices of others who have studied similar processes or groups, and their own situated voices.

Unlike in the approach to information literacy and research often taught in general educational courses that focus on information literacy, fieldworkers do not attempt complete objectivity, do not divorce themselves from their relationship to the systems they are studying. Rather, fieldworkers engage in a process of what ethnographer Hortense Powdermaker calls stepping in and stepping out, examining the culture from the perspective of both an engaged participant and a detached observer. As Bonnie Stone Sunstein and Elizabeth Chiseri-Strater argue in their textbook, FieldWorking, fieldworkers "conduct an internal dialogue between [their] subjective and objective selves, listening to both, questioning both."[37] Fieldworkers continually question themselves—What surprised me? What disturbed me?—in order to articulate how their own beliefs and assumptions shape their understanding of what they observe. As fieldworkers, students engage with information ecologies through participation as insiders, trying on what it feels like to be an integral part, while also engaging through critical analysis as outsiders, trying to understand the culture by seeing it in relationship to their knowledge and values beyond that particular context.

This dual status as both insider and outsider epitomizes the experience of service learning. Through their work with a community partner, students begin to experience what its is like to be a member of that organization. At the same time, their participation and membership are necessarily partial. Their engagement with the organizational information ecology is brief and incomplete, and students must balance their roles as contributors to the ecology and as learners within the academic culture. Fieldwork provides a structure for productive reflection on this tension, and field writing provides a mode of sharing the resulting understanding within and beyond the community.

Because fieldwork puts the researcher within the frame, field writing emphasizes the cultivation of a strong narrative voice to a greater extent than most other types of academic research writing. Fieldwork is generally written in the first person, because "to ignore yourself as part of the data distorts your findings." Writing in the first person "allows you to write with your own authority and with the authenticity of your own fieldwork, and it will ensure your credibility."[38] Writing with a strong, personal voice enables students to claim the authority without qualifications that Weinberger sees as central to being persuasive to communities beyond the academy, particularly those mediated by the Internet. Practicing to acknowledge and embrace their own values and relationships in their writing may prove more useful to students in using information effectively in settings beyond the classroom than a presumption of detached neutrality. Like the online writing that Weinberger values, field writing also has a strong narrative flavor. Strong field writers make skillful use of think descriptions of character, action, and setting to trace the path of activity over time as its components intersect to focus on what's surprising and interesting.

Field writing, rich in voice and story, is more likely to be interesting to people who are members of information ecologies beyond the academy than the dry, dense prose that is often encouraged in traditional research writing. The values implicit in fieldwork differ from those behind information ecology in one respect: Inquiry in fieldwork focuses on understanding cultures as they are; information ecology frames inquiry as part of a process of empowering the system to make changes that improve it. However, because its style creates interest, fieldwork reports are likely to be powerful conversation pieces for engaging members of an information ecology in strategic questioning.

Integrative Activities

In order to center the course on the metaphor of information ecology and the methods of fieldwork, with the service learning context shifting from a peripheral to a primary site for intellectual engagement, I designed four new major assignments. Students now begin the semester by composing an information technology autobiography. During most of the course, their work focuses of two fieldwork projects, one examining a virtual information ecology and the other examining even more closely the site of the student's service learning project as an information ecology. At the end of the term, students compose a final portfolio, which includes a revised version of the information technology autobiography and a variety of samples of work from their fieldwork, through which they demonstrate how their semester's learning experience has moved them toward a more personally engaged approach to the use of information and technologies throughout their lives.

In their information technology autobiographies, students are asked to reflect on their experiences using information and technology up to the beginning of the course and the values that inform their related choices. Students answer such questions as: What does it mean to be information and technology literate? How does use of information and technology impact your lifestyle? What technologies do you consciously choose not to use, and why? The assignment was adapted from technology autobiography assignments developed and used successfully in computers and writing classes by several colleagues from across the country, particularly Karla Kitalong, Tracy Bridgeford, Micheal Moore, and Dickie Selfe.[39] At the end of the semester, students revise their autobiographies to reflect their enhanced understanding of the role of information and technology in their lives. Because an autobiography is fundamentally a story, the conventions of the genre compel students to begin crafting strong narrative voices.

In the virtual fieldwork assignment, students investigate an online information ecology using the fieldwork methodologies. We spend several weeks in class learning fieldworking techniques, such as taking fieldnotes, conducting interviews, closely analyzing discourse, and producing think descriptions and adapting them to the online environment through extensive prewriting and group discussion. Exercises from FieldWriting provide an important starting place for this work, supplemented by examples of fieldwork focused on virtual cultures and collaborative exploration of online environments within the networked classroom. The virtual fieldwork assignment also includes a traditional annotated bibliography of secondary sources. In their field writing, students practice balancing their own voices, those of their informants from within the virtual ecology, and the voices of other researchers discovered through traditional library and online research techniques.

Through peer reviews of drafts and class discussions, students compare what they have discovered, gaining a richer picture of a range of authentic online contexts of information use. Students investigated such diverse online ecologies as George Mason students building and maintaining networks of friends on Facebook, people seeking sexual partners on Craigslist, recent Ethiopian and Eritrean immigrants sharing information on a discussion board, and players crafting identities within World of War, a massively multiplayer online game. Several students chose to investigate social networking sites, including Facebook, MySpace, and Friendster. The differences that students discovered in their research between these environments and between the different groups of people using them led to highly productive discussions. Students' observations about the management of privacy, identity, and relationships both confirmed and complicated previous research on these themes as represented in the course readings and the secondary sources they referenced.

In the second half of the semester, students put the fieldworking skills they have begun to develop through the virtual fieldworking assignment to work in analyzing the site in the community in which they are conducting their service learning projects as an information ecology. Rather than being solely devoted to the service learning project, the forty-five hours students invest in order to receive an experiential learning credit for the course are divided into thirty hours of service learning and fifteen hours of additional fieldwork research on-site. The service learning project was previously a largely individual project isolated from both the intellectual core of the class and the larger work of the organization. Coupled with the experiential learning fieldwork, the project is now transformed into an opportunity to investigate information use in their community site as an information ecology and to see their project as part of that larger system, contextualizing their use of information and technology within the activity of the organization. Students take detailed notes on what they observe about the work of the community partner, reflect on their response to these observations and on their own participation, analyze the material and technological environment in which the activity takes place, interview participants in the organization, and examine documents and artifacts that mediate the use of information within the information ecology. In their reports, they describe how the organizations' people, practices, and values work together as a system, how they have coevolved over time, and how they do or not reflect a healthy diversity. Through their fieldwork, students may identify misalignments and poor fits between elements in the system that can serve as the basis for conversation about how to change it. Students share their findings with leaders of the community partner in hopes of launching such dialogs.

In the fall of 2005, students worked with a wide variety of organizations across Northern Virginia. Several students worked in schools, observing how students, teachers, and administrators learned to use information and technology in elementary school computer labs, in social studies courses, and in automotive technology shops. Through sharing their observations and drafts, they discovered how differently the dynamics of information use played out, even in what they had assumed to be very similar educational settings. Students worked with senior citizens and new immigrants in public libraries, exploring the interface between the role of the Internet in the lives of the users of the library with whom they worked closely and traditional culture of information practices to which librarians were committed. They discovered how the public policy context of the work of environmental research organizations moved its activities beyond what was covered in their science courses. They examined the role of everything from e-mail lists, bulletin boards (physical and virtual), and seating arrangements in shaping collaborative, deliberative processes in honor committees and medical offices.

In a final portfolio, students develop visual representations of their learning in the course, building hypertextual concept maps drawing connections between ideas from the course, such as coevolution, situated identity, embodiment; course goals, such as understanding information ecologies and fieldwork techniques; New Century College's competencies, such critical thinking and aesthetic awareness; and samples of their work, including both finished, formal assignments and drafts and notes from throughout the semester. The final portfolio also includes a revision of the technology autobiography and an introductory essay in which students project forward, examining how what they have learned will impact their future decisions about the discovery, evaluation, and analysis of information using its supporting online technologies.

Through the metaphor of information ecology, the methodology of fieldwork, and a set of integrative activities, students in the new NCLC 249 examined and enhanced their information literacy in a manner more consistent with the goal of personal engagement than in past semesters. By investigating information use in their own lives and in diverse virtual and organizational environments, paying close attention to the dynamics of distributed activity and interrelations of people, tools, techniques, and values in the process of change, students equip themselves to put their information literacy into practice in the multiple, rapidly changing contexts that will confront them in personal, academic, professional, and civic lives. Although a systematic analysis of the outcomes of this first offering is beyond the scope of this piece, my students' performance suggests that significant gains were made in all three kinds of engagement. Not only did students' portfolios offer strong evidence that they were leaving the course more personally engaged than when the semester began, but their evaluations of their service learning and the comments on their work with their community partners submitted by their supervisors also demonstrated a more reciprocal and intensive public engagement. More than in any undergraduate course I have taught, students at all levels of ability went beyond the requirements of the formal assignments, consulted with me outside class, and engaged in extensive, substantive revision, all suggesting an increase in traditional student engagement as well.

Although a closer look at the student learning in NCLC 249 over several offerings of their new curriculum is needed to tease out what in this design might be useful elsewhere, I offer it here as example of how I am working to address the limitations of narrow conceptions of information literacy and the pedagogical practices that often accompany them. Overcoming these limitations is a challenge that should be shared by the developers of any general education curriculum that makes teaching through a fully engaged approach to information literacy a goal. Without overselling my working solution, I offer my process of engaging the problem as a starting point for others taking on this challenge.

Notes

1. George D. Kuh, *The National Survey of Student Engagement: Conceptual Framework and Overview of Psychometric Properties* (Indiana University Center for Postsecondary Research and Planning, 2003. Available online from http://nsse.iub.edu/pdf/conceptual_framework_2003.pdf, 1.

2. George Kuh et al., *Student Success in College: Creating Conditions That Matter* (San Francisco, CA: Jossey-Bass, 2005).

3. Edward Elmendorf, Travis Reindl, and Maurice Williams, "Stepping Forward as Steward of Place" (Washington, DC: American Association of State Colleges and Universities, 2002).

4. Ernest L. Boyer, *Scholarship Reconsidered: Priorities of the Professoriate* (Princeton, NJ: Carngie Foundation for the Advancement of Teaching, 1990).

5. Barbara Jacoby and Associates, *Service-Learning in Higher Education: Concepts and Practices* (San Francisco, CA: Jossey-Bass, 1996).

6. IUPUI English Department, *Iupui English Department* (2001). Available online from http://english.iupui.edu/.

7. Association of College & Research Libraries, *Information Literacy Competency Standards for Higher Education* (Chicago: ALA, 2005. Available online from http://www.ala.org/ala/acrl/acrlstandards/informationliteracycompetency.htm.

8. Genie Tyburski, *The Virtual Chase: Criteria for Evaluating Information* (Ballard Spahr Andrews & Ingersoll, LLP, 2004). Available online from http://www.virtualchase.com/quality/criteria.html.

9. Jean Lave and Etienne Wenger, *Situated Learning: Legitimating Peripheral Participation* (Cambridge: Cambridge UP, 1991); Etienne Wenger, *Communities of Practice: Learning, Meaning, and Identity* (Cambridge: Cambridge UP, 1998).

10. Julian E. Orr, *Talking about Machines: An Ethnography of a Modern Job* (Ithaca, NY: Cornell University Press, 1996).

11. Louis Menand, *The Marketplace of Ideas* (American Council of Learned Societies, 2001). Available online from http://www.acls.org/op49.htm.

12. Hugh Burkhardt and Alan H. Schoenfeld, "Improving Educational Research: Toward a More Useful, More Influential, and Better-Funded Enterprise," *Educational Researcher* 32, no. 9 (2003).

13. Library of Congress, *The Digital Future* (C-SPAN, 2004). Available online from http://www.c-span.org/congress/digitalfuture.asp.

14. David Weinberger, *Small Pieces Loosely Joined: A Unified Theory of the Web* (Cambridge, MA: Perseus Books, 2001).

15. Ibid., 122

16. Ibid., 92

17. Ibid., 141

18. John Seely Brown et al., *Storytelling in Organizations: Why Storytelling Is Transforming 21st Century Organizations and Management* (Burlington, MA: Elsevier, 2005).

19. Weinberger, *Small Pieces Loosely Joined*, 128

20. Ibid., 144

21. Edwin Hutchins, *Cognition in the Wild* (Cambridge. MA: MIT Press, 1995).

22. ACRL, *Information Literacy Competency Standards for Higher Education.*

23. Paul Duguid, "Material Matters: The Past and Futurology of the Book," in *The Future of the Book*, ed. Geoffrey Nunberg (Berkeley, CA: University of California Press, 1996).

24. David. M Levy, *Scrolling Forward: Making Sense of Documents in the Digital Age* (New York: Arcade Publishing, 2001).

25. Ibid., 71

26. Christine Bruce's research similarly treats information literacy as embodied experience and defines its dimensions based on her observations of that experience. See Christine Bruce, *Seven Faces of Information Literacy* (Adelaide, South Australia: AUSLIB Press, 1997).

27. Levy, *Scrolling Forward*, 58

28. Bonnie A. Nardi and Vicki O'Day, *Information Ecologies: Using Technology with Heart* (Cambridge, MA: MIT Press, 1999).

29. Ibid., 34

30. Ibid., 14

31. Ibid., 14

32. Ibid., 58

33. Ibid., 68

34. Ibid., 56

35. Ibid., 53

36. Ibid., 53

37. Bonnie Stone Sunstein and Elizabeth Chiseri-Strater, *Fieldworking: Reading and Writing Research, 2nd ed.* (Boston: Bedford/St. Martin's, 2002), 9

38. Ibid., 46

39. Karla Kitalong et al., "Variations on a Theme: The Technology Autobiography as a Versatile Writing Assignment," in *Teaching Writing with Computers*, ed. Pamela Takayoshi and Bryan Huot (Boston: Houghton Mifflin, 2003).

Learning, Engagement, and Technology

Joan K. Lippincott

This chapter focuses on new ways of thinking about promoting information literacy, engaging students, and building community in technology-enabled environments, both physical and virtual. Whether or not a campus has a formal "learning communities" program, libraries can play a role in enhancing community development in the context of teaching, learning, and information literacy. The chapter discusses some innovative current practices and explores two arenas with as yet unrealized potential for uniting technology use, social learning, and student engagement: virtual spaces, such as simulated environments and virtual worlds; and new types of physical, technology-enabled learning spaces.

Learning Communities

Many researchers who have studied the nature of learning have concluded that a social process involving interaction with, and observation of, others is an important component of learning. In the 1960s, some pioneers in higher education began a movement to establish learning communities within colleges and universities in an effort to combat the isolation of students in their academic lives and to create an environment where students engaged each other and faculty in sustained conversations about academic subjects. Typically, students in this established learning community model take a group of courses together so that they get to know each other and feel comfortable interacting with their peers. In addition, this learning community model sometimes includes a residential component in which students live together in the same dormitory in addition to taking a group of courses together. In some cases, these learning communities are limited to freshman-year experiences; in other cases, they extend into later years of students' campus experiences.[1]

New Learning Communities

As the learning communities movement developed, it focused on in-person, social interaction in the context of curriculum and was disconnected from the increasing use of technology on campuses. In fact, in the early years of Internet use on campuses, technology was often thought to isolate students, rather than build community, and there did not seem to be an obvious link between learning communities and technology. However, some faculty, librarians, and information technologists understood the potential for incorporating technology into the curriculum in a way that would enhance community rather than isolate students. In 1994, the Coalition for Networked Information, with its partners, the Association for Research Libraries and Educom, initiated a program called New Learning Communities (http://www.cni.org/projects/nlc/), which brought together pioneering teams of institutional partners who were developing programs emphasizing learning, community building, and use of technology. Although the types of programs being developed were not necessarily learning communities in the traditional sense (a common set of courses coupled with residential community), the programs selected to participate in the 1995 and 1997 New Learning Communities workshops sought to increase interaction among students and between students and faculty through the use of technology in the curriculum.[2] An example of one program that was part of the New Learning Communities initiative was the Freshman Interest Group program of the University of Washington's UWired program (http://www.washington.edu/uwired/). This program combined a small group freshman experience, incorporation of information literacy into the curriculum, and the design of new, collaborative spaces that featured group use of technology.

Net Gen Students

Although the UWired program and others provided an innovative connection between technology and the curriculum, in the early and mid-1990s, most students used technology on the periphery of their education, writing papers, using word-processing software, searching online catalogs and databases, and exchanging e-mail, but not "living" online. However, by 2000, when the Net Gen students (students born between 1982 and 1991) arrived on campus, the manner in which many students perceived and used technology had changed dramatically.[3] Today's students do not see use of technology as something separate or special; cell phones, desktop computers, laptops, PDAs, and IPods or similar devices are part of their lifestyle and culture. Many students use these technologies in a social, community-building way, for example, moving easily between talking with friends in a cafe while instant messaging others who are not physically present and including them in the conversation. However, innovative use of community-building technologies within the curriculum is still not the norm. Faculty and librarians used technology in the curriculum primarily to post information, to present Powerpoint™ slides in a lecture or lecture–discussion format in class, and to conduct e-mail exchanges. For the most part, these are static, limited information-delivery functions or one-to-one communications.

Information Literacy

Within higher education, librarians have been relatively early adopters of technology. Even before the Internet was widely used in libraries, information literacy programs in the mid-1980s began to incorporate use of computer technology into the objectives taught in class sessions. Librarians began to teach students to search databases on their own (previously librarians had searched databases for their users) and to use online catalogs. The databases were either accessed via computer modem, often with per minute charges attached, or via CD-ROM, which usually meant simultaneous access was limited to a very small number of users. Today, librarians still emphasize the searching process in their information literacy sessions, widening the focus to databases and other resources licensed or owned by the library as well as resources available in the broader Internet. Other topics in information literacy education include evaluating information, managing research information effectively, and understanding its ethical use.

Although librarians develop information literacy programs that interact with specific courses, their role in the class is generally that of guest lecturer and they are not seen as a member of the class's "community." Some students may take the initiative to contact the librarian who instructed them after the class as they work on their assignments, but usually students are advised that they can consult with any librarian and do not need to seek out the one who met with their class. In emphasizing efficiency, librarians may be losing an opportunity to build a sense of community within the course. In addition, librarians usually teach students to search for information with the implicit assumption that searching is an individual, not a group, process, pairing students only if there are not enough computers for each student to have an individual workstation. There is little emphasis or encouragement of the kind of peer consultation that today's students frequently use to learn new technology skills. Librarians' teaching style also may reflect the faculty member's course structure and his or her assumptions about learning, such as whether working with other students on assignments is academically honest.

Christopher M. Hoadley and Roy D. Pea wrote: "an effective learning community is a knowledge-building community of practice, one in which members of the community interact to collaboratively help other individuals and the group to increase their knowledge."[4] Learning communities emphasize the notion that each member, including the faculty member, can learn from other members of the community. There is less emphasis on the teacher as sole expert than in traditionally taught courses. This distinctive assumption about the learning environment could provide the foundation for information literacy programs by developing mechanisms to give students more of a role in teaching, and not just learning, about information. Today's students work in groups both formally, as a part of course assignments, and informally, blending the academic and social aspects of their lives. Giving students a more central role in the learning process related to information literacy might result in their becoming more invested in learning about information topics. For example, librarians could train one student or a small group of students in a course to be the information literacy experts for that course and those students would be available online to assist their classmates. If some formal class instruction were needed, the trained student(s) could conduct an overview in a computer lab and then provide time where the other students explore resources while they circulate to assist students who need help. A librarian could be on hand physically or via chat to answer questions that were beyond the students' expertise.

In another model, learning communities could be supported throughout the semester via an online presence by a librarian in the environment of a course management system. The early concern that the Internet would isolate people and encourage individuals to spend many hours alone has not been supported by evidence. The authors of a Pew Internet & American Life survey in 2001 concluded: "the online world is a vibrant social universe where many Internet users enjoy serious and satisfying contact with online communities."[5] In courses that actively use a course management system such as Blackboard™ or WebCT™, or in distance education courses, librarians could establish a presence beyond posting and linking lists of library resources appropriate to course assignments. For example, they could offer "office hours" at critical dates during the semester, write a blog that suggests resources or offers pointers on research, develop social bookmarking services, or participate in a class discussion board. These are all mechanisms that have the potential to foster the development of community among class members in the virtual environment.

Implications for Integrating Technology, Information Literacy, and Needs and Preferences of Net Gen Students

As libraries contemplate the direction of their information literacy programs, develop new services, and renovate or build new spaces, they can explore how the interplay of physical and virtual spaces, new technologies, content, and services can be molded into an information environment that is responsive to the needs of Net Gen learners. Will libraries develop genuinely innovative programs that embrace new ways of making themselves a more integral part of the teaching and learning environment, or will they merely modernize traditional ways of serving their users?

Games

In higher education circles, when the topic of gaming comes up in discussions of learning with technology, it is sometimes dismissed quickly because of a misunderstanding of how the term *gaming* is generally used in the educational context. Many adults immediately conjure up visions of violent games that promote antisocial behavior, and though such games are a large part of the entertainment market, there is growing recognition that computer games designed for educational purposes have a potentially important role to play.

Students enjoy computer games for a variety of reasons, and many are congruent with the principles of deeper learning.[6] For example, games are engaging, they draw students into a situation, such as a crisis in a simulation, that may have connections to real-world situations. Students gradually build skills during the playing of games, which is the type of contextual learning advocated by the National Academies in their report *How People Learn*.[7] The students have to apply the skills they have learned in one context to a different context. Today's students like active learning, and a problem-solving environment is ideal for them. They like progressing to higher levels of mastery and receiving rewards, even if the reward is some type of virtual icon. When games are played in a group, they also incorporate the benefits of collaborative learning. Although not referring to games per se, George Kuh and his colleagues wrote: "this pedagogical approach [active and collaborative learning] is positively and significantly related to all areas of student engagement and all measures of what students gain from their collegiate experience."[8]

Others have extolled the virtues of games in the context of learning more directly. One author writes that good teachers "know how to engage and motivate students to pay attention, and to keep focused for long and productive periods on specific learning activities. In this regard, videogames are unparalleled. Providing intense multimodal experiences that blend near-photorealistic 3D graphics, animation, and sound effects, videogames are powerful problem solving and guided discovery tools."[9] He writes further that although some educators question the value of games, they need to understand that the game interface is just the "motivational engine" that encourages students to delve deeply into the system, encouraging them to develop skills and knowledge.

Of the learning objects specifically designed to develop information literacy, TILT, the game show–style online tutorial developed at University of Texas, Austin library (http://tilt.lib.utsystem.edu/) is the best known. This tool is designed to develop basic information literacy skills as students step through a series of questions with visuals (for example, spinning wheels) typically used on television game shows. The underlying concept of this gamelike tutorial is to engage learners in a fun exercise while teaching some basic skills that are not particularly engaging alone. Other academic libraries have adapted and adopted the TILT game for their information literacy programs.

TILT was designed for use by individuals, but a new generation of information literacy games could be designed for group discovery and learning. Because many Net Gen students like working in groups and enjoy tangible (or virtual) rewards for their success in games, information literacy game developers could develop a mode where the game is played by small groups within a class or by different sections of large courses, where those with high scores would win some type of prize. The developers of an agricultural economics game used in the twelfth grade asked students to recommend improvements to the prototype, and the students suggested that the game be more of a competition. The developers revised the way they implemented the game, holding a competition between school teams and providing prizes for those who achieve a high profit and a high "goodwill" score.[10] Use of games in a group context can build community while enhancing information literacy skills. The element of competition itself can promote the team identification aspects of community.

Simulations

Another type of gaming activity is the use of computer simulations in education. This is the area where the most development and progress are occurring at the higher education level. Many of the simulations being developed for higher education emphasize teamwork as part of playing the game. Simulations are usually problem-solving activities, where students are presented with a situation related to the topic being studied and given instructions on their task(s). As they progress through the simulation, they are given further instructions until they reach the end. Some simulations involve periodic group or class conversations to assess what has been learned up to that point before going on to next steps. Resources for games suited for the academic market are M.I.T. PDA Participatory Simulations Site (http://education.mit.edu/pda/index.htm) and the Woodrow Wilson Center for International Scholars' Serious Games Initiative (http://www.seriousgames.org/about.html).

Libraries could become more involved in the world of games and simulations in a number of ways. They could develop simulations that involve searching for information resources, accessing and evaluating them, and creating bibliographies. They could involve realistic environments of the library building and the library's interface to online resources. Development resources and a high level of expertise. Today's college students expect rich and complex graphics, not amateur productions. Although developing stand-alone simulations for an individual library does not seem to be a realistic option for most institutions, it would be possible for a consortium or other group of universities to pool resources and develop an information literacy simulation. Another possibility would be to engage partners to develop simulations for particular content subsets (for example, a business resources information literacy simulation). The James Madison University Libraries, in partnership with the university's Center for Instructional Technology and Center for Assessment and Research Studies, is reconfiguring its information literacy tutorial into a gaming format; the game will focus on health sciences.[11]

Another promising avenue for libraries to become involved with simulations is for them to actively work with institutes, companies, and individuals developing simulations for particular content areas, such as engineering, business, environmental science, history, or literature. As part of the set of tools available for problem solving in these virtual environments, a link to the library, a set of selected digital library resources, or a guide developed by librarians for the content area could be integrated into the simulation and thereby promote use of high-quality information resources as part of the problem-solving process. For example, in a simulation where students have to determine the cause of an environmental contamination and recommend a course of action to ameliorate the situation, they could be guided to resources that had chemical information, public safety information, and other types of resources. One challenge in developing this kind of learning tool is being able to create the right kind of balance between close guidance—through presentation of preselected resources—and scaffolding, which encourages students to find information in a more open-ended search process.

Virtual Worlds

A newer arena that libraries could use to become involved in gaming is the realm of virtual worlds. Unlike simulations, which generally follow a narrative and emphasize problem solving with a clear beginning and end point, some virtual worlds are environments that focus on the establishment of subcommunities in which various events or communications take place. An example of this type of virtual world is the very large-scale (often referred to as "massive") multiuser virtual world called Second Life (http://secondlife.com/), which was featured at a conference on gaming and education at the National

Academies.[12] One can join this virtual world free of charge, although some advanced services involve payments. In this environment, individuals take on a virtual persona, called an avatar, and appear on the screen as that character. An individual's character can take various actions, including building virtual spaces that are virtual representations of the physical world. For example, members of Second Life have developed newspapers, memorials, fundraising events for survivors of natural disasters, virtual book signings, and a library. At present, this library serves as a venue in which members of Second Life can deposit their own writings. It is a collection of creative output, which is valuable, but only one aspect of a library.

Academic librarians should create opportunities to create more robust libraries that offer services and interactions in virtual worlds. These environments appeal to Net Gen students because the worlds have rich visual content, are active (characters do things), and are social, involving virtual interaction that is sometimes blended with in-person contact. For example, some students take their laptops and get together in someone's dorm room to play in virtual worlds together while they simultaneously interact with individuals who are not in their physical location. Students seem to thrive in these environments that blend individual and group activity, and in-person and virtual social interactions. Librarians would need to understand which virtual worlds their students tend to join and whether they would be suitable venues for library presence. Then, librarians would need to determine what types of services they could offer, how they would represent them visually, and how they would staff them. Although this approach might not appeal to a wide range of academic libraries, those that serve a student population that tends to heavily populate virtual worlds may wish to explore this avenue for delivering services. This might be similar to the way the Internet Public Library (www.ipl.org) operates, but rather than setting things up so that users need to go to a separate location and actively seek out the library, the library would be right there in an environment where they spend time. There is room for experimentation in the delivery of library services and information literacy education, and it would be of great value to the library community if even a small number of libraries experimented in the virtual world arena and reported their results.

Learning Spaces
Technology also has implications for shaping libraries' physical environments.

Libraries can reconfigure space in a number of ways to promote a sense of campus community and to enhance the delivery of information literacy instruction. Many libraries are undergoing renovations and expansions to address the changes they need to make in their physical facilities as the result of developments in technology (for example, pervasiveness of Internet and wireless communications use, increased interest in active learning, and the blending of social communication and academic work in library facilities). Frequently, the changes to address these factors result in libraries planning information commons or learning commons for their facilities. These spaces include workstations with more extensive software than was typical in most reference rooms, staff that are trained to assist with both content and technology questions, and work areas configured for group use in addition to the traditional single-person workstation furniture. Moreover, new learning spaces can foster a sense of community by displaying the work products of faculty, students, and staff, through either display of artifacts or virtual displays of digital productions.

Learning Spaces for Group Use

Libraries are adapting to the norms of Net Gen learners, who have a propensity for working in groups. This group activity may combine actual academic work with intermittent socializing both with friends who are present in the physical space and those who are accessible via instant messaging, cell phone, etc. Students often like to work in groups even when they are not all working on the same assignments, trading bits of information, and enjoying companionship. Traditional libraries have emphasized quiet spaces for individual study, and most librarians and users agree that a proportion of library space needs to continue to serve that traditional function. However, libraries are adapting to the need for a portion of their space to be configured for group use.

A variety of configurations can address the needs of group work, and it is generally useful to have a number of options for group work in one facility. For example, some students like to gather on soft furniture such as sofas and armchairs while discussing next steps in taking on a group project. With wireless access, they can easily access course management systems, library resources, Internet resources, the faculty, and friends. A cafe in the library can serve the same purpose and also provide refreshment. Many libraries are dispensing with the "no food in the library rule" and establishing cafes in their buildings.

Many information commons include group study rooms, which often have a central worktable, white boards, and various types of equipment such as a computer and a projector. Other group rooms may be set up as practice presentation spaces, where students can practice presenting a talk at a podium and invite their friends to sit in the "audience" and critique their performance prior to their actual presentation in class. Other group spaces offer high-end multimedia production equipment so that students can develop multimedia products for their course assignments or campus activities. Some group spaces also may be large tables or work spaces in an open area, if noise is not an issue and quiet spaces are available on other floors. Stanford Meyer Library offers an innovative collaborative service called TeamSpot in an open area of the library (http://academiccomputing.stanford.edu/teamspot/). Students connect their laptops in a collaborative space and are able to each make modifications on a large screen shared display. The facility was specifically designed to support group, problem-solving work. All these types of learning spaces encourage students to interact in the context of their academic work and, as a byproduct, promote a sense of community and belonging.

Learning Spaces for Information Literacy Instruction

Information commons or other areas of the library frequently incorporate some classroom space for information literacy sessions or other types of classes. In designing or renovating these classrooms, flexibility is key as technologies and preferred teaching methods are in flux. Tables and chairs with wheels are readily available in the market and provide maximum flexibility. Classrooms with movable tables can be changed quickly from lecture format, all facing forward, to group work style, with chairs on all sides. Classrooms with white boards on at least three walls can be rearranged without regard to which orientation is the true front of the room. With flexible spaces, librarians may be encouraged to incorporate large segments of group work, in which students actively learn as they pursue information for their course-related assignments during information literacy sessions.

Learning Spaces for Multimedia Production

Some libraries incorporate multimedia production units into their facilities, and they may operate as a separate entity within the library or be integrated into some services, such as information literacy programs. Multimedia production offers new opportunities for librarians and other information professionals to teach students about a wide range of topics, including searching for existing information as background for projects; finding images, sound files, and moving images to incorporate into projects; working with multimedia software; and developing projects that are academic in quality and not just entertaining. Many students produce multimedia productions as course projects because they are specifically required by the faculty or, more commonly, because they choose to express themselves in this medium. Working with students in this arena provides particularly good opportunities for librarians to educate students about intellectual property issues, in the context of students as users of information produced by others, and as creators of products that will be used by others. If multimedia production units are outside the library administratively, librarians should seek opportunities to collaborate with the individuals who provide workshops or other instruction in this area, offering to add their skills and knowledge to sessions with students and/or faculty.

Spaces for Learning Communities

Although most information commons are planned with the overall needs of the campus community in mind, one university planned such a facility with a component that specifically addresses the needs of the institution's learning communities program. At the University of Kansas, a group was charged with developing a plan for a collaborative learning environment (physical space) that would also improve information and technology services. Included in the planning group were representatives from the campus's freshman learning communities initiative because the learning community groups had difficulties "finding a place to gather where they could study, discuss ideas related to their particular theme, work on assignments together, or interact with faculty outside the classroom."[13] Parts of the facility were designed to provide the needed community spaces. This information commons space was developed in a former computer lab and not in the main library. In a related outcome, the committee found that although the freshman program of collaborative communities existed, few faculty teaching only upper-level courses were familiar with the goals and principles of collaborative learning, and they instituted some faculty workshops to develop a greater awareness and adoption of the learning communities principles among faculty.

Taking Steps

Overall, addressing information literacy needs today requires some fundamental rethinking about the librarians' and library's role in learning. Learning communities focus on every participant's capabilities to be both teacher and learner. This requires some reorientation in the pervasive model of information literacy, where the librarian is the clear "faculty expert" to a new model where the librarian learns about information seeking and production from students as well as contributes knowledge to the class. Making a commitment to change requires resources, particularly staff time. One suggestion for beginning the change process is to have each librarian involved in information literacy instruction develop a relationship with one course in which the librarian's goal is to become a member of that learning community for a semester. Ideally, the course chosen would have a faculty member who incorporates active and collaborative learning styles into the class, gives assignments that require outside information resources, and is open to partnership with a librarian.

Libraries could assign an individual or small group to begin to study and participate in games and virtual worlds in order to understand what might work for their campus community and how the games and virtual worlds might be used to incorporate information literacy components. Ideally, the individual would consult with or work with students, or if a small group is assigned the work, it should include some students.

Libraries that are early in the planning process for renovations of facilities, and therefore have years before the facility is ready, or those that have no funds for renovation can begin to plan incremental changes that could have an important impact. Rearranging existing furniture to provide designated space for group work, installing cafes, or buying inexpensive comfortable furniture in an area with wireless access can help the library contribute to developing a sense of community within the institution.

Conclusion

Libraries can use technology in development of services, information literacy programs, and facilities to foster learning communities. New opportunities exist to enhance the library's participation in campus learning communities through the use of gaming in the curriculum and the provision of newly configured social spaces. Librarians can seek opportunities to become involved in existing campus learning communities and use them as venues to incorporate information literacy instruction while learning from students themselves about their use of technologies and information. With new configurations, librarians can provide learning spaces that encourage active, collaborative learning and give students access to the wide range of technologies they need to work in today's learning environments. Libraries and librarians can continue to play a vital role in students' learning if they evolve their services and facilities to incorporate features that engage twenty-first-century learners.

Notes

1. Barbara Leigh Smith, "The Challenge of Learning Communities as a Growing National Movement," *Peer Review* 4, no. 1 (summer/fall 2001). Available online from http://www.aacu-edu.org/peerreview/pr-fa01/pr-fa01feature1.cfm.

2. Joan K. Lippincott, "Learning Communities for Excellence," *College & Research Libraries News* (Mar. 2002).

3. Diana Oblinger and James Oblinger, "Is It Age or IT: First Steps towards Understanding the Net Generation," in *Educating the Net Gen*, ed. Diana and James Oblinger. EDUCAUSE, 2005. Available online from www.educause.edu/educatingthenetgen/.

4. Christopher M. Hoadley and Roy D. Pea, "Finding the Ties That Bind: Tools in Support of a Knowledge-building Community" (2003). Available online from http://www.ciltkn.org/knresearch/tiesbind.html. (Note: To appear in K. A. Renninger and W. Khumar, eds., *Building Virtual Communities: Learning and Change in Cyberspace* (New York: Cambridge University Press).

5. John B. Horrigan, "Online Communities: Networks That Nurture Long-distance Relationships and Local Ties," Pew Internet & American Life Project, Oct. 31, 2001. Available online from http://www.pewinternet.org.

6. Colleen Carmean and Jeremy Haefner, "Mind over Matter: Transforming Course Management Systems into Effective Learning Environments," *EDUCAUSE Review* 37, no. 6 (Nov./Dec. 2002): 26–34. Available online from http://www.educause.edu/ir/library/pdf/erm0261.pdf.

7. National Research Council, *How People Learn: Brain, Mind, Experience and School* (Washington, DC: National Academies Press, 2000). Available online from http://www.nap.edu/catalog/9853.html.

8. George D. Kuh, Thomas F. Nelson Laird, and Paul D. Umbach, "Aligning Faculty Activities and Student Behavior: Realizing the Promise of Greater Expectations," *Liberal Education* (fall 2004).

9. Joel Foreman, "Videogrames and Good Teachers: The Similarities. The Possibilities," *Converge Online* (2005). Available online from http://www.convergemag.com/story.php?catid=2318storyid=95685.

10. Leti M. Bocanegra and Margie Harrison-Smith, "The Agricultural Economics Challenge: An Online Program Where High School Students Learn Economics and Agriculture of the Salinas Valley," *First Monday* 10, no. 6 (June 2005). Available online from http://firstmonday.org/issues/issue10_6/bocanegra/index.html.

11. "James Madison University (JMU) Libraries: Grants and Acquisitions," *C&RL News* 66, no. 11 (Dec. 2005): 834.

12. "Challenges and Opportunities in Game-based Learning," The National Academies Center for the Advancement of Scholarship on Engineering Education, Conference in Washington, DC., Nov. 2, 2005. Available online from http://www.nae.edu/nae/caseecomnew.nsf/weblinks/NFOY-6HXRHX?OpenDocument.

13. Susan M. Zvacek and Scott Walter, "High-velocity Change: Creating Collaborative Learning Environments," *EDUCAUSE Center for Applied Research Bulletin 2005*, no. 15 (July 19, 2005). Available online from www.educause.edu/ecar/.

Contributors

Darren Cambridge is Assistant Professor of Internet Studies and Information Literacy in New Century College at George Mason University. Prior to coming to George Mason, he served as Director of Web Projects at the American Association for Higher Education and National Learning Infrastructure Initiative Fellow at EDUCAUSE. An internationally known expert on electronic portfolios, Cambridge has led the development of the ePortfolio Specification for the IMS Global Learning Consortium, served on the Board of the Open Source Portfolio Initiative, directed development of the Learning Record Online assessment system, and facilitated EDUCAUSE's Virtual Communities of Practice initiative. He is Associate Director of the National Coalition for Electronic Portfolio Research, facilitator of EPAC International, and co-coordinator of George Mason's Multimedia Minor program. Making his home in Washington, DC, he is active in the Washington Interfaith Network.

Jo Ann Carr is the Director of the Center for Instructional Materials and Computing for the School of Education at the University of Wisconsin Madison where she coordinates information and technology services for the school's teacher education programs. She has been involved in information literacy activities for almost twenty years as a member of state and national committees on K–12 and higher education information literacy. In September 2003, she coauthored, with Ilene Rockman, "Information Literacy Collaboration: A Shared Responsibility" published in American Libraries. Jo Ann has presented workshops on information literacy at American Library Association and Association of College and Research Libraries conferences as well as for the numerous universities and library consortia. Jo Ann has served on writing teams and committees for information literacy issues for the

Wisconsin Department of Public Instruction, the Association of College and Research Libraries and the Wisconsin Association of Academic Librarians.

Jim Elmborg has been an Assistant Professor in the School of Library and Information Science at The University of Iowa since the fall of 2000. Before that time, he was an academic librarian, most recently in South Carolina as the Andrew Mellon Librarian for Information Technology at Furman University and Wofford College, and before that Head of Library User Education at Washington State University, Pullman. Elmborg's research deals with information literacy in general and its implementation in library practice specifically. He is the author of several articles, including "Teaching at the Desk: Toward a Reference Pedagogy," winner of the ACRL Instruction Section's Publication of the Year Award for 2003. He has recently finished co-editing *Centers for Learning: Writing Centers and Libraries in Collaboration, Publications in Librarianship no. 58*, published by ACRL.

Randy Burke Hensley is the Student Learning Programs and Services Librarian at the University of Hawaii at Manoa. He is responsible for developing programs and services that enhance the ability of undergraduate students to understand, appreciate, and perform original research. He is also responsible for developing initiatives that will heighten the role of the library on campus as a place of individual and group activity for teaching and learning. His previous positions include Assistant Head, Odegaard Undergraduate Library, University of Washington, and Social Sciences Librarian, California State University, Chico. He is currently a member of the Immersion Faculty of the ACRL Institute For Information Literacy, has served as Chair of ACRL's Instruction Section, and is the recipient of the 2002 Miriam Dudley Instruction Librarian Award. His current research interests are undergraduate research instruction, student engagement, and active learning.

Adianna Kezar is Associate Professor at the University of Southern California in the Higher Education Administration Program. She was formerly a faculty member at the University of Maryland and at George Washington University. She has over 75 published articles, books, and chapters on the topic of leadership, governance, and change and innovation. Her work has been featured in top-tiered education journals including *Journal of Higher Education*, *Review of Higher Education,* and *Research in Higher Education.* She is well known for her book entitled, *Understanding and Facilitating Organizational Change in the 21st Century*, (Jossey Bass, 2001). Correspondence may be sent to kezar@usc.edu.

Joan K. Lippincott is Associate Executive Director of the Coalition for Networked Information, a joint project of the Association of Research Libraries (ARL) and EDUCAUSE. Some of the programs for which she has provided leadership within CNI include New Learning Communities, Assessing the Networked Environment, Working Together (emphasizing collaboration between librarians and information technologists), and Learning Spaces. Prior to joining CNI in 1990, Joan was a librarian at Cornell, George Washington, Georgetown, and SUNY Brockport. Joan is chair of the editorial board of *College & Research Libraries News,* and she is on the board of the Networked Digital Library of Theses and Dissertations. She has written articles and made presentations on the topics of teaching and learning with technology, learning spaces, information commons, net gen students, networked information, electronic theses and dissertations, and institutional repositories.

Pat Davitt Maughan has facilitated, since fall 2002, a campus-wide collaboration of campus academic partners in all planning associated with the annual Mellon Library/Faculty Fellowship for Undergraduate Research and its attendant faculty institute. The fellowship and institute represent important steps on the UC Berkeley campus in transforming the undergraduate curriculum by working with faculty, educational technologists, instructional designers, other academic support, and administrative units to design research assignments and learning experiences for students that foster independent discovery through use of library print and digital resources. Pat's early career was devoted to science librarianship; from 1982–1991 she served as Engineering Librarian, and later as Head of the Science Libraries at the University of California, Berkeley. She now serves as Project Manager for the Mellon Library/Faculty Fellowship for Undergraduate Research and Berkeley Library's User Research Coordinator for Doe and Moffitt Libraries.

She is a consultant to the California Digital Library in Oakland and a former Townsend Center Fellow in the Humanities at UC Berkeley. Pat's current areas of interest include library research instruction, assessment of student learning, and program evaluation.

Katherine C. McAdams is Associate Dean for Undergraduate Studies at the University of Maryland, College Park. She began her career in education as a high school teacher in the early 1970s, then worked as a journalist. She has been teaching college journalism and communication courses since 1979. Dr. McAdams holds three degrees from the University of North Carolina at Chapel Hill: a bachelor's degree in English education, a master's degree in journalism, and a Ph.D. in communication research. She and her Carolina colleague Jan Johnson Yopp are co-authors of *Reaching Audiences*, a best-selling introductory text in college journalism. She has published, presented, and consulted widely on effective communication and on journalism education. Winner of three university-wide teaching awards, Dr. McAdams has been at the University of Maryland since 1987. She served for five years as executive director of College Park Scholars, a nationally recognized living–learning program, and she has been Associate Dean of Undergraduate Studies since July 2005.

Nancy S. Shapiro, Associate Vice Chancellor for Academic Affairs at the University System of Maryland, directs the USM K–16 initiatives and co-chair of the statewide K–16 Partnership for Teaching and Learning. She works with thirteen public institutions of the USM, two-year colleges, and K–12 schools to foster critical partnerships and learning communities to improve the quality of teaching and learning for Maryland's teachers and students from kindergarten through college. Prior to joining the University System of Maryland, Dr. Shapiro directed the freshman writing program at the University of Maryland and served as the founding director of the College Park Scholars Program, where she designed and developed the first interdisciplinary living–learning programs at the university. She has had extensive experience in undergraduate education reform, including research, teaching, and administrative leadership roles in composition and rhetoric, writing across the curriculum, faculty development, and general education. She is the principal investigator of a five-year National Science Foundation

Math Science Partnership grant, and is currently engaged in a study of the impact of MSP funding on reform of undergraduate teaching and learning, assessing change, and sustainability in higher education. In addition to the NSF MSP projects, she is the principal investigator and director of two Title II Teacher Quality Enhancement Grants designed to build high school and college learning communities to prepare future teachers for urban schools, with special emphasis on science and mathematics teachers. Her publications include three co-authored books, *Creating Learning Communities* (Jossey Bass, 1999), *Sustaining Learning Communities* (Jossey Bass, 2004), and *Scenarios for Teaching Writing* (National Council of Teachers of English, 1996); numerous articles and reviews on a variety of undergraduate education topics, and an edited collection of essays on K–16 statewide initiatives, *Metropolitan Universities* (fall 1999). Dr. Shapiro serves on the editorial boards of two journals, *Liberal Education* and *Communication Education*.

Margit Misangyi Watts earned degrees from the University of Michigan and the University of Hawaii. Dr. Watts is the Director of Manoa Educational Partnerships through which she strives to create intellectual and practical synergies between educational constituencies as well as the wider community. She is the author of two books—*High Tea at Halekulani*, a study of feminism and clubwomen, and a textbook for first-year students, *College: We Make the Road By Walking*. As a scholar she has also contributed to the discourse on the impact of technology on teaching and learning and the challenge of student engagement. Dr. Watts is also viewed as a leader in the creative integration of information literacy into traditional college curriculum. As a past director of two programs for first-year students, she brought national recognition to the University of Hawaii through her classroom teaching, program leadership, and scholarship.

About the editor

Craig Gibson has been Associate University Librarian for Public Services at George Mason University since 1996, where he is responsible for public services, instruction, and liaison and outreach programming for four campus libraries. He has also been a part-time consultant in the university's Department of Instructional Technology Support Services. Previous positions include reference and instructional positions at the University of Texas–Arlington, Lewis-Clark State College, and Washington State University. Since 1996, he has taught as an adjunct faculty in the graduate library science program at The Catholic University of America, offering courses in information literacy, reference service, and use and users of information systems. He has given numerous presentations and workshops on critical thinking, information literacy, and the learning library, and has written articles on critical thinking, assessment, and distance learning. Since 1999, he has been a member of the ACRL Immersion Program, a summer institute designed to train librarians in information literacy pedagogy, assessment, programming, and leadership. He was a member of the ACRL Task Force on Information Literacy Competency Standards for Higher Education and wrote the introduction to the standards. He was Member-at-Large in the ACRL Instruction Section and was selected to participate in the Instruction Section's Think Tank III, for which he co-authored a paper on assessment of information literacy skills. Since 1996, he has been a member of, and recorder for, the National Forum on Information Literacy. His current research interests and professional activities focus on student engagement, information literacy as cultural practice, and liaison and outreach programs for academic libraries.

Index